How to Save Your Marriage
by Becoming a Better Man

By Hunt Brown

Some might argue that this is a work of fiction. For the most
part it isn't, but any person place or thing in the book that might
co-exist in the real world is used fictitiously and only for
purposes of illumination and education.

A quick caveat: it is written by a man, for men, but pronouns are
fungible things. If it works, use it, regardless of your gender or
sexual orientation.

http://www.betternmanbettermarriage.blogspot.com

INTRODUCTION

This is why your marriage is ending: you've come to realize she is never going to change.

You haven't had sex since who knows when. It seems every conversation turns into an argument, and every argument, no matter how it begins, turns into an argument about the same things, things you thought was settled long ago. She is cold and unresponsive and is suspicious of your motivations. She has hurt you in so many ways you have already disengaged, decided she is something to be endured, to be dealt with, but not someone you want to love and you know she doesn't love you anymore. You are so tired of fighting that if she asked for a divorce, you'd agree just to be done with it. You feel trapped.

You will admit to your share of mistakes, but the truth is she is unreasonable, emotional, and at times bordering on crazy. Plus, she's not willing to do her share. You're willing to meet her halfway on a lot of issues but you have to see movement on her part first.

This is why you are still married: you dread the thought of a divorce. You don't want to fail. You told yourself from day one that you would not get divorced. Your self-worth is involved. Child support, property division, alimony, attorney fees, all spell financial ruin for you. You don't want to lose the kids. At some level the marriage works for you. Maybe it's negative, inertia, but it could be worse.

This is why you are reading (hopefully buying) this book: you don't know what you want. You are clueless; you are rudderless on a stormy sea; you are alone in a very large and impossibly dark room. Some part of you thinks that maybe being married is better than being divorced, that if she were to change it could all be, if not great… at least good again

And here is the truth of the matter: you can save your marriage. You can find purpose, you can take charge of your life, you can turn on the lights. Not only that, you can be happy. You can live life to the fullest, and you can become a man that others admire and seek for counsel. You can be a leader, and you can find success and fulfillment beyond your wildest imagination. And you can have a happy, loving marriage. I shit you not.

Before we get started on exactly how that will all come to pass you need a little reality check.

This is why she thinks the marriage is ending: she's come to realize you are never going to change. You haven't had sex since who knows when. It seems every conversation turns into an argument, and every argument, no matter what how it begins, turns into an argument about the same things, things she thought was settled long ago. She sees you as cold and unresponsive and thinks you are suspicious of her motivations. She has been hurt by you in so many ways that she has already disengaged, decided you are something to be endured, to be dealt with, but not someone she wants to love. She believes you don't love her anymore. She is so tired of fighting that if you asked for a divorce, she'd agree. She feels trapped.

She will admit to her share of mistakes, but the truth is you are unreasonable, emotional, and at times, bordering on crazy. Plus, you're not willing to do your share. She's willing to meet you halfway on a lot of issues but she has to see movement on your part first.

She is still married to you because she dreads the thought of a divorce. She doesn't want to fail. Her self-worth is involved. She told herself from day one that she would never get divorced. Divorce means financial ruin for her, and …. It could be worse.

Let me spell it out for the slower readers: she is just as confused as you are. She is just as desperate, just as lonely, just as abandoned, and hurt. Just like you she sees herself as the victim; just like you she feels she has done all she can do.

You are both in a burning house each pointing at the other, knowing the other started the fire, and neither of you are going to lift a finger to put it out until the other does the same. The house is going to burn to the foundations and the divorce lawyers are going to rake through the ashes for your remains.

Unless, of course, you do something.

Don't wait for her, don't expect her to help. (And don't blame her for not helping, for doing nothing, for acting exactly like you were.) Act to put out the fire, and then start repairing the damage. Depending on where she is she may help, and that will be a good thing. She may never help, and you may end up selling the house, but your interests (equity in the analogy, spiritual in reality) will be protected and you will get more out of it than you would if you'd let the house burn.

PREFACE

I put the preface after the Introduction because I didn't want you to read it until after I'd caught your attention. This book is different from anything you've read, anything on the market. I've tried to put the hay down where the goats can get at it, so the book is, at times, irreverent and profane, and often profound.

A little house keeping[1].

First off I have to give respect where respect is due. As you read this book, you might find yourself thinking…. *This guy, he's on to something here*…well, I am. But to paraphrase Isaac Newton, if I see a little farther than you, it's because I stand on the shoulders of giants.[2]

The first of my giants is Harville Hendrix. Really, he's done all the heavy lifting here: he designed the compound pulley; I'm just tugging on the rope. He wrote "Getting the Love You Want," and he conceptualized one of the key tools this book will give you, Mirroring. Don't worry what that's all about right now[3], we'll get to it, but we'll only get to it because of Harville. While you're here at the store you should slide on down past the "G" section to the "H" section and you will find his cannon somewhere between Harley and Hyman. You could pick anyone

---

[1] Assuming you've decided to put out the house fire.

[2] Nanos gigantum humeris insidentes. At the time monographs and treatises were written in Latin.

[3] Normally when I refer to something somewhere else in the book, I'll footnote the chapter, but don't worry about Mirroring right now. Trust me. We'll get to it.

of his books and you'd be fine, but pick "Keeping the Love you Find."

The second of my giants are Bob Patterson and Sulaiman Nuridan who crafted the concept of "The Clearing."[4] These men have been my mentors and my friends. Every thought in this book was wrought in Bob's basement with their help and the help of the other men in The Clearing. Bob and Sulaiman made the concepts of Imago tangible and real. They are the Kesuke Miyagi to my Daniel Laruso.[5] Seriously, Google these guys.

For the purposes of this book you are YOU, your wife is MARY and you both tend to speak in **bold** and think in *italics*.

I do have friends, but when I refer to a friend (or wife) in this book it's not a reference to a specific individual, but to an amalgam of experiences coalesced into one or another proto-pal. Or as my friend Sgt. Friday might say, the stories are true, but the names, fact patterns, circumstances, sexes, family components, and timing have all been changed.

Marriage is synonymous with relationship, as is divorce with "break up," A lot of guys who are reading this book have not elected to take full advantage of the tax laws of this great nation, and a few can't. Don't get hung up on it.[6]

You'll notice that at the end of the book there is no worksheet with instructions for you to list the pleasures and pains of your relationship. Nor is there any instruction here for you do it. This book isn't about convincing you that everything is good, that you should cleave only to happy thoughts. There is no

---

[4] Epilogue
[5] Karate Kid, Columbia Pictures, 1984
[6] See the caveat on the copyright page

homework; there are no nifty exercises that are going to bring sudden enlightenment and joy. Life doesn't work that way.

Throughout the book you will come across parables. They may seem out of place, odd, even irrelevant. Don't skip them. They are there for a purpose.

Additionally you'll probably notice that some of the earlier chapters refer to material in the later chapters. I wish I could make being a better man linear, with simple steps from A to Z, but it's more like a geodesic dome, made of triangles joined at the corners. Every joint is essential to the structure, so to with becoming a better man. It's made of a bunch of parts that interconnect and which are dependent upon each other to form the whole. This means to get the full value of this book you might have to read it three or four times, you might even have to use bookmarks.

All the numbers here, all the percentages, are rule of thumb and are based upon my synthesis of the books and web sites in the bibliography, along with countless seminars, sessions, and discussions with knowledgeable types. If you need exact numbers please feel free to do your own research, but understand that if you are bunged up over the numbers you are not getting the point of the book. You might want to take it back and see if you can get a refund.

Finally, I'm not telling you what to do. I'm telling you what I did, what works for me. For the purposes of marketing I am supposed to be a font of wisdom, a sage, a Mr. Fix-it. I'm not. I am for the most part just like you with two small exceptions.

The first is I took the time to write this book. John D. MacDonald wrote in the preface to King's "Night Shift," "If you want to write, you write." It was the best advice I've ever taken,

and I will share it with you in more detail later in the book.[7]
Having said that, nothing in here is original.

I had a friend who had read "The Secret" and he called me after
reading it and screamed: "What a total load of crap!"... or words
to that effect. He couldn't believe people would buy into the
philosophy behind the book. I told him, and I'll tell you now,
that the key is finding a format, a protocol, a voice to which you
respond. Almost every self-help book ever written will say
essentially the same thing: think positively; listen actively;
communicate honestly; act responsibly. Done and done.

My friend obviously did not resonate with The Secret. All fine
and good, lots of people did, do and will. There wasn't a
problem with the book, and there wasn't a problem with him, it
just wasn't the right book for him. So I recommended another
and another until he found one that made sense to him. This
book, with its unique voice and approach, may be your cup of
tea, it may not.

The second way I'm different than you is that I have been there
and done that, and I spent a lot of time grappling with why my
marriage of twenty-three years failed. The easy answer was to
blame the cancer, the patronizing answer was that she needed
space, but the real answer is that, no matter what the
contributing factors were, I dropped the ball.[8] I wasn't the sole
cause of the breakup, but I played my part in it and had I acted
differently, had I known then what I know now, it might not
have ended.

The Japanese have a concept; actually it may just be Toyoda,
called Kiazen. The idea is that if a manufacturing enterprise pays

attention to its mistakes and learns from them it will consistently improve in efficiency and productivity. I think it applies in life as well, if you pay attention to your mistakes, own them and learn from them, you will constantly improve the quality of your life.

Toyoda takes it a step further and runs an assembly line faster and faster until something breaks. Once they figure out why it broke, and fix it, they crank it up and run it yet faster again. Thus failure is essential to long term success.

Marriage is a stress test. It will pop your rivets, snap your welds, and uncoil your springs. Re-riveting, re-welding, and re-coiling only serve as temporary maintenance. Kaizen says find the problem that allows the rivet to pop and fix it, the run it through the test again just to see what breaks next.

Right now, you may think the assembly line that is your marriage is broken and shut down for good. Kaizen says it's not even close to that. Yes, you've run the factory into the ground, but that's a good thing. At the very least, you know where the problems are.

I looked at my failed marriage and my life, saw where my problems were and said I can do better. I can be a better man.

I wrote this book to better understand where I am in my journey to be a better man. I am a work in progress. You are a work in progress.

Here's a thought for you: when all you have is a hammer, all your problems look like nails. Get ready for some new tools.

Chapter 2

Getting married is easy. It's socially acceptable. Your parents are proud of you. There are parties, congratulations and presents involved. It's unifying. People smile a lot. And hey, guess what? Someone else is paying for it. The best part: hope. Hope for the perfect union, the unlimited future, the kids, the vacations, and the chance to be an adult, to step into the role you have been auditioning for your entire life.

Getting divorced is a nightmare. It's socially acceptable only to, at a maximum, half the people you know. The rest will take her side. Your parents are disappointed in you. It's divisive. There are no parties, no congratulations and guess what? You get to pay for it. The old rule of thumb is multiply the cost of the wedding by three. The worst part: hopelessness. The future is fraught with uncertainty. You have failed at a very important undertaking. Anger and recrimination overwhelm every thought. And worse, you end up acting like a kid.

The bottom line is that everyone who is married would rather have a good marriage than a divorce, and yet over 50% of all marriages end in divorce.

Here's the skinny: roughly 41% of all first marriages end in divorce before the eighth anniversary; 60% for the second, and 73% for the third. The good news out of that is this: 40% of the people who got a first divorce didn't get a second.

The cynic says they got lucky the second time around, but my take is that the guy who is the three or four time loser is the guy that's making the same mistakes over and over again. The 40%

that made the cut the second time were the ones that learned from their mistakes and didn't repeat them: they became better men.

And that's not "better" as in some proto-feminist Alan Aldaistic[9] wimpy way. They still like football, drink beer, fart, burp, and curse, but they became better communicators, better listeners, they became more honest, more authentic, and without a doubt, happier. They became better men. The pity is (and I speak from experience here) it took a failed marriage, a divorce and years of misery to get them there.

The goal, here, is to give you the skills that 40% latched onto before your marriage is over.

And if, God forbid, you are already separated, take a speed reading course. 60% of separated couples get divorced within a year, and it seems directly proportional to the time apart. 5% don't survive one month, 10% don't make it past two, etc.

If you are separated and you want to save your marriage, start now. Literally, get out your phone, dial her number and when she answers (or you roll over into voice mail) say these words.

I am sorry. I know that any apology is inadequate, but I had to tell you. I realize how important you are to me and I have decided to change, to become a better person, a better husband. I don't know exactly how right now because I'm only on the second chapter of the book, but I want you to know that I love you and to let you know you will see a change in me.

---

[9] No offense intended to Mr. Alda, a great writer and actor.

If you won't do the above, just put the book back on the shelf, pick up your coffee and go Google "divorce attorney."

Most couples divorce for simple reasons: Toxicity; One has grown, the other hasn't; One or both give up[10]

Toxicity

Well adjusted people will leave a toxic relationship. A toxic relationship is, at its simplest, one in which involves addiction or abuse. Co-dependent and enabling behaviors keep a toxic relationship going. It is easy to make excuses for the other's behavior; it is easy to value the toxic partner's deep need for support; it is understandable how the victim can find meaning and value in suffering.

If you are in a toxic relationship, you cannot save your marriage. You haven't got a marriage to save until the toxic issue is addressed and resolved. If your wife is an alcoholic, drug abuser, or is inclined to abuse you, either emotionally or physically, you cannot and should not save that marriage, but you may save your life and maybe your children's lives by stepping up to the plate and stating that the toxic behavior is unacceptable: it has to stop.

If the toxic partner reforms, maybe this book will help you get yourself and the marriage back on track. Don't kid yourself, though. It isn't going to be easy. She's going to need help. Alcoholics Anonymous, anger management, or some other program, but so are you. It's a relationship, remember? Both of

---

[10] But what about betrayal? What do we do about cheaters? - Most affairs are the result of a failed marriage, not the cause, and that's dealt with in Chapter 7. The exception to that rule is those who are congenitally unable to remain faithful and that is akin to addiction.

you are involved. You didn't create the problem, but your behavior has kept you in the game, and as Dr. Phil would say, you're getting something out of it. You need the support of Alanon or some other co-dependent support group that will help you recognize your contributions and find the strength to change your behavior.

If the toxic partner will not reform and the behavior continues get the kids and leave. If you have the time, buy the book before you leave because the book will still help you through your next relationship.

One has grown

The one that has grown most probably is not you, but we'll go over it anyway.

There is plenty of evidence that we are attracted to someone that is as evolved and emotionally mature as we are. The 36 year old guy hitting on 18 yr old girl is not the some kind of studly Dali Lama, he is immature. The girl probably has some issues of her own if she's interested in the 36 year old, so figure their emotional age is around fifteen.

I had a teacher once who urged everyone in her class "always associate with people who are smarter than you." Her belief was that hanging with better students would inculcate better study habits, a deeper thirst for knowledge, and a greater appreciation for education. She never explained why any "smart person" would want to associate with those she encouraged to befriend them.

Aphorisms find their origins in truth. Birds of a feather do flock together, water does find its own level, and it does take one to know one. The woman you chose to bed and wed was, at that moment, in everyway your equal in maturity, enlightenment and growth.

It is in the human nature to grow, to explore, and to mature. It is also in the human nature to coast and take it easy, so our emotional and spiritual growth comes in fits and starts. Even trees do this. Look at the mighty oak tree and it's easy to think its magnificence is the result of steady consistent yearly growth, but the rings will show a different story, with decades of compact, thin rings showing little growth, and individual thick rings of rapid growth.

In relationships we tend to push and shove each other through growth, we are each an anvil on which the other has forged their emotional evolution and maturity. But sometimes, if growth is too painful, if the truth that needs to be faced is ignored, growth stops in one, and yet continues in the other. In some instances, the trauma of the death of a loved on can lead to insight for one partner and denial for the other. When one partner grows and the other doesn't the relationship will end as both will become dissatisfied.

It's the same with music or sports. As your skills increase you seek partners with the same skills. Roddick might consent to give you a lesson in tennis, but he's never going to ask you to play or to be his doubles partner. So, too, when one partner has out grown anger and self-victimization the other must do so as well or the relationship will not survive.

I have a friend who lived in a volatile relationship. He and his wife were given to extremes in argument. One day he realized he didn't like what anger did to him. He didn't like the physical sensations: the racing pulse, the burn of adrenaline, the blood pressure, the tension. He also didn't like the person he was when he was angry, the way he behaved, the things he said, and the things he couldn't un-say. Most importantly, he didn't like that by his behavior he was teaching his son to act the same way.

He decided to change. He learned to control his reactivity, he learned tools that invited discussion, he learned how to defuse situations, he learned how to examine his anger, find the fear, and let it go. (Don't sweat it, we'll get to the "how" later in the book.[11])

His wife didn't get it. She was stuck in her reactivity. She continued to shout and scream, to blame, to manipulate. She tried to egg him into arguments. In other circumstances her behavior might have changed too, but perhaps she was too conditioned by the behavior of her parents, or was too fearful of change to let go of her anger.

Eventually he said "enough." He left. His departure was the crisis she needed to begin to change. She had two choices. Stay as she was and lose him, or change to keep him. Her growth point was not in her anger… might have been if she'd kept up with him. Her growth point was in realizing that her behavior had adverse consequences, and that the tool of anger was no longer useful. Learning to let go of non-productive and counterproductive behavior is the first step in personal growth. Last I checked they were getting along pretty well.

The point of that story was that my friend grew and until his wife decided to get on board they were headed towards divorce.

If you picked up this book it is not because you are the one who has grown. Let go of the false pride now and take ownership[12] of

---

[11] I'd give you the chapter, but for now just accept it and read on.
[12] Chapter 5

where you are. There is the chance that your spouse has grown past you, and if so this book can help you catch up.

Both give up.

This is probably the reason for ninety-nine percent of all divorces and failed relationships. It's gone sixteen rounds and there is no decision. It's triple overtime, and everyone is exhausted.

The couple got into bad habits, they fostered resentments, they withdrew, they abandoned trust, they didn't listen and they projected their feelings onto the other. Neither recognized the opportunity for growth and blamed the other for creating the problems.

The truth is eighty-percent of your relationship with your wife is fine. It's the remaining twenty percent that's driving you both bonkers. Pain resonates across time; pleasure endures only in the moment.

Consider the last time you smashed your toe into the bedstead, or slammed your thumb with a hammer. Just evoking the memory can cause your heart to beat faster, you eyes to wince as if in pain. This is a survival skill. It comes from the old brain, the reptilian stem[13]; it is a talent that allowed your greatest of all grandfathers to learn not to stick his foot in that new thing called fire. Pain is part and parcel of damage. Pain is the reminder to avoid things that damage our body and shorten our life. We remember pain so we do not have to experience it again.

---

[13] Chapter 6

Pleasure, on the other hand, is fleeting. It has to be pursued and experienced. Oddly, this too is a survival skill. Pleasure is the carrot to the stick of the biological imperative. If sex wasn't fun, if it didn't feel good, it wouldn't get done, and if it did it would be done infrequently and unlikely to preserve the species. On the other hand, if your greatest of all grandfathers could recall in exacting detail with full sensation his top three orgasms he would never leave the cave. Who would? Thus the transitory nature of pleasure is essential to the propagation of the species.

So, too, you remember the pain in your relationship and it overshadows the pleasures. One burst of anger can obliterate countless smiles. A moment of hurt will echo through time and occlude hours of joy. Just as your greatest of all grandfathers learned not to stick his foot in the fire, you have learned not to go there, you have learned not to share fears, you have learned not to trust, not to appreciate, not to enjoy because experience has taught you it leads to pain, betrayal, recrimination, blame and anger. It makes it hard to remember the laughter.

If you accept the premise that eighty percent of your relationship is good, you have to wonder where it's coming from, and the answer is that there is the very real chance that the wonderful, caring, loving, fun, exciting, daring beautiful woman you married still exists, but your perception of her has changed. You don't need to underline that last sentence or fold down the page, when it becomes important I will bring it up again.

At the end of the day, after all the extra innings, after all the pain that obscures the joy, one or both simply say "there has to be a better way, there has to be someone out there that will be easier to live with, there has to be someone out there who will love me and I've come to realize I'm never going to find it in this relationship." So they give up. They walk away from the game with time on the clock.

Here's the sad thing: both are going to do it again. Whatever their mistakes were, they didn't recognized them, they didn't fix them, and they are doomed to keep making them in their next relationship. (Remember, 60% flub their second marriage, 73% the third.[14]) Until you learn to close the face of your club you are going to hook the ball. Until you step through the ball in tennis, your return is going to be haphazard. No one ever improved their game by hoping it was going to get better.

This is probably you. It's probably your wife too, but she's not here, we're not talking about her, and accept the fact that you cannot do one thing to change her. This not the Matrix[15] and there is no pill that will bring her to a clear understanding of the wonder that is your reality.

Here is what you must do: you have to analyze your behaviors honestly, identify the areas that need improvement, and then go about the hard work fixing yourself.

If you do that, and you do it well, there are three possible logical outcomes:

ONE: Maybe you grow to find yourself in the second situation above, where you have changed but she cannot. Net result: divorce, but you feel better about yourself and are more than likely to be in the forty percent that don't get divorced the next time around;

TWO: Maybe you are the laggard and once you catch up you find yourself engaged in a new and vibrant relationship that is

---

[14] Can you imagine three divorces?
[15] Warner Brothers, 1999

based on growth, respect, and (as far fetched as it may seem) love;

THREE: Most likely, you both have work to do, and your work will lead (lead as in leadership) inexorably to her growth, and as you both grow you find yourself in a new and vibrant relationship that is based on growth, respect, and (as far fetched as it may seem) love;

Three for three, all good.

The corollary to all this is that if you do nothing, if you pitch this book and reaffirm your belief that you are good enough and it is all her fault, there are three possible logical outcomes.

ONE: You will continue to suffer in a loveless marriage.

TWO: You will get a painful divorce, fall in love again, make the same mistakes again, and as sure night follows day you will get the same result, a loveless marriage or a divorce.

THREE: You live alone and die alone.

Three for three, all bad.

DO THE MATH.

THE ROWBOAT

We are in a rowboat, sitting side by side on the middle thwart, each in control of an oar. As with all rowboats, we are facing the stern so most of the time we have no idea where we are going. She's got her goals, maybe I have mine. As long as we're in sync it's fine.

And we used to be in sync. When we first got in the boat it was great. We went places, and when we got bollixed we laughed about it. But now…

Some times she'll look over her shoulder and see some goal that is clear to her but completely out of my view and tell me I'm rowing too fast, or too slow or what ever. Sometimes I'll do my best and pull right along with her. But sometimes, a lot of times, depending on my mood (have we been having a good time, do I feel frustrated, am I happy) or how she said it (that tone that implies I can't row…)   I'll pull so hard it jags us off course one way, not change at all, or maybe even slow down. Sometimes just because I don't like being told what to do I'll simply row backwards so we spin madly, going nowhere at all. And sometimes, most of the time, I know she's doing the same thing, and if she's not trying, why should I?

Not surprisingly this doesn't work well for her, and honestly it doesn't do me any good either. Worse, it comes to pass that no matter what I say I'm going to do, even when I really try, she suspects (sometimes believes, worse knows) that I'm not rowing right so when we don't get to her goal, no matter how much I've tried, it's my fault.

And more to the point, drifting around aimlessly on the water isn't satisfying at all. It's hot. We get bored. We get thirsty. We get cranky and it's always the other's fault. After a while it begins to make absolute sense to abandon a perfectly good boat and hope for the best. Maybe another will pick me up. Maybe I can swim it. Maybe I'd be happier under the water.

So I got a couple of choices. Jump in the water or continue on as-is are two, but neither hold a lot of appeal. The problem seems insurmountable, a no winner. The only remaining choice seems to be to do exactly what she wants, and friends that isn't going to happen, for a lot of reasons. Pride. The natural order of things. Stubbornness. The fact that nine times out of ten I am right when it comes to rowing decisions. The fact that she's never going to change her rowing either.

Really, why should I abase myself by doing exactly what she wants? Didn't I go through this once before? Why should I do it again?

Anyway, we're rowing along and I see a place I think we should go. But I don't mention it because I don't want all the hoopla and recriminations that come with a course change. I never get there, we never get there, and I figure it's mostly her fault.

So we're rowing along, making all the effort but getting nowhere, really. But it's not so bad. We're getting along. I'm lost in my thoughts, she in hers, when I look over my shoulder and I see a point she's always been talking about and I wouldn't mind reaching, but we're not on course for it.

But by now I've got a feel for how she strokes and I'm thinking if I just adjust my stroke ever so little, I can actually direct us there. If I just back off when she does, pull a little harder here, scull a little there, I can put us to her goal.

So I do, and of course she likes it, she got she wanted and (of course) no thanks to me, so I get bummed and decide that's the last time that's going to happen.

So it's back to the oars and more of the same o' when I start thinking that if I adjust my stroke to hers and get what she wants, it figures I can do the same and navigate to my goal. No fighting, no telling anyone what to do, just adjusting the old stroke. So I look over my shoulder, figure where to go and get to it. Before long bingo, we're there.

So I'm happy and she's kinda happy and I pick another spot and badda boom, just by adjusting my stroke we get there too, and I'm happy and she's getting upset that were just hitting my way points, so I listen to her, put my new skills to get us to her point (which actually wasn't a bad way point, I enjoyed it.)

And I'm thinking this is pretty good. I'm not caving to her at all, I'm actually the one in charge, and that feels good, but it doesn't feel great.

Then one day we're rowing along, I'm doing my thing, guiding us along, when I notice she's making it easier. She's pulling harder. She sculling and giving the boat direction, and now we're heading to points not only in double-time, but we're having fun to boot.

Was that just too transparent? Your marriage is the rowboat. Adjusting the stroke is change. Work on it.

CHAPTER 3

TO BE A BETTER MAN CLEAN UP YOUR SIDE OF THE STREET

If she would change, your life would be better. If you want to make your life better it follows you must change her, but alas, brother, you can't.[16]

But the good news has been around since the beginning of time, and was first cogently propounded by Newton's Third Law: for every action there is an equal and opposite reaction. If you change, she will. If you lead, she will follow.

In 1982 criminologists James Q. Wilson and George Kelling proposed in an Atlantic Monthly article, Broken Windows, that criminal activity was an opportunistic response to neglect and apathy. They theorized that if a broken window on a street remained un-repaired, people would assume that nobody cared and soon more windows would be broken, and the lack of repair would invite further degradation, graffiti and trash would appear, and the street would devolve into a "bad" block. Just as one bad thing leads to another, the environment would steadily worsen as it became more inviting to criminal activity. Their theory is that to effectively fight crime we must first fix the broken windows.

This theory has been put to the test in both New York City and in Los Angeles, and studies have shown it to be true. Litter begets litter, squalor invites crime.

---

[16] Lord knows you have tried to change her and failed.

This is true in relationships as well. The worse she acts, the worse you act. If she gets angry and stomps around the house then many men will feel permitted to do the same. Door slam is met by door slam.

Here's the logic I want you to follow: 1) I want to be a better man; 2) I know areas that I can improve; 3) I will improve.

Here's the logic most of you are following: 1) I want to be a better man; 2) I know areas that I can improve; 3) I'm not going to do a damned thing until she does.

I can understand the second set of reasoning. It is tough to make an effort when you feel the other is not pulling their fair share. You want equality and fairness, and damn-it, you didn't make this mess all own your own, why should you be the one to clean it up?

The problem with the second set of reasoning is that it is self destructive. Imagine your marriage is over' you are divorced: would you then want to make yourself a better man? If you didn't have to deal with the horrid inequality, baiting, and manipulation you endure every day could you find the impetus to grow?

If your answer is yes, then why wait? Your growth, your improvement is its own reward. And here is the thing: your growth will lead to her growth. Just like the criminologists theorized, if you clean up your side of the street conditions will improve, she will improve. She'll start replacing windows and painting the trim. (Metaphorically: don't expect her to start shopping at Home Depot)

But why should I have to go first? Think back to the burning house analogy: someone has to act. You've got the book, you've got the tools, you've got the skills. Right now you are the only one who CAN act. But if that's not enough, don't think of it as going first: think of it as getting a head start.

And if she doesn't follow? If you do all this work and her side of the street is still rife with crack whores, pimps and needles? Move on. You're a better man; you'll find a better woman.

A quick caveat: "cleaning up your side of the street[17]" is defined as incorporating all the elements of being a better man into your life. It is not simply picking your underwear up and replacing the toilet paper after you've emptied the roll. If you cherry pick a few easy improvements and then say "ah, well, I did my part"... Hell. Just sent the book back and I'll refund your money. You can't become a better man if you act like a child.[18]

Quick analogy: before every commercial aircraft locks its brakes and spools up its engines the flight crew have performed a bit of kabuki whereby they have explained all about exits, seatbelts and oxygen masks. The key to remember, if you are seated next to a child, is to don your oxygen mask before helping the child don his or hers. The reason is very simple. If you pass out from lack of oxygen the child will not be able to help you, even if you succeeded in placing the mask on the child's face: not good for you, possibly not good for both of you.

If however, you put your mask on first, you will be able to assist the child, whether or not the child is conscious: good for both of you.

By the same token, in your life, get your own oxygen mask on first. Only after you have taken care of yourself can you hope to

---

[17] I attribute this vital concept to Bob Patterson.
[18] Cold but true

be of assistance to anyone. It's not a perfect analogy, but it's worth thinking about.

So, how do you get our oxygen mask on first, how do you clean up your side of the street? You don't have to NOT DO any thing. This isn't about deprivation, this is about improvement: Kaizen.

What you do to clean up your side of the street is to take positive and intentional steps to make yourself a better man.

CHAPTER 4

TO BE A BETTER MAN BE A MAN FIRST

When you ask most guys who they are they will tell you their profession. This makes sense if you have Mitsubishi tattooed on you ass and you are a robot that welds automobile frames on an assembly line. It was what you were made to do, it is all you know to do, it is all you have to do, and it is all you can do. It makes no sense for a man. As a man you have countless roles to play, you are a father and a child, a husband, and employee, a boss, a spiritual creature and at times, hopefully, a satyr. You are a sportsman, you are a philosopher; you are a student and a teacher.

I was a trial lawyer for a long time[19]. I was very good at analyzing fact patterns, finding logical inconsistencies and discovering the lies that pointed directly to the truth. I asked incisive questions, and I remembered every half-truth, every innuendo, and every tacit reservation. You truly did not want to sit across the table from me during a deposition. I took no prisoners.

Unfortunately, these skills did not translate well into my marriage. My wife did not appreciate it when I cited to her earlier contradictory statements, nor she did not like the way I parsed her answers or the way I cross-examined her to elicit the facts. Truly, at times, she didn't want to sit across the dining room table from me because… I took no prisoners.

---

[19] Hence the footnotes.

My skills at litigation worked great for me at the office, and to a certain extent with my professional friends, but they did not do spit for my marital relationship, and if anything these incredible money making skills undermined the foundations of my wife's love for me. I hope the irony isn't lost on you. The very skills that made the money that provided the life I thought she wanted destroyed the relationship and drove her out of my life.

My communication skills, wrought by litigation, did not help me in my relationship with my family, nor did they help me understand my relationship with God and the universe, neither of which appreciate being cross examined. In point of fact, everything that I had studied and trained to become professionally did absolutely nothing for me as an individual.

When I was sworn in as a lawyer, it wasn't until death do us part. I didn't pledge, as I did on my wedding day, that I (unlike my parents) would not fail in this undertaking. I did not swear to love, honor and obey the law[20]. I did not pledge my troth to blind justice.

It was an important day, but it wasn't as important as the day I stood before family and friends and committed myself to my wife, and yet I seemed powerless to prevent the lesser from overwhelming the greater.

Long after she left I realized that I had my cart before my horse, I was paying my club membership before my mortgage, I had my priorities mixed up. In an epiphany it came to me that if I wasn't happy as a person then I wasn't going to be happy as a lawyer. If I wasn't the best man I could be, I couldn't be the best husband, so it all came down this.

---

[20] Okay… I did swear to obey the law.

Be a man first, a husband second, a father third and a professional fourth.

If you are going to do anything well, you have to know yourself, you have to know who you are, your weaknesses and your strengths. You have to bring the complete package to the table. You have to be not just a man, but the best man you can be.

Second, a husband. Your wife, your partner, is the anvil of your growth. You were drawn to her, you love her, because she makes you face the areas in which you need to grow, just as you do for her. It's driving you crazy right now, but here's the truth: she, or someone very much like her, is essential to your growth as a man. And, as you will come to understand, if you address those areas, the craziness will go away. In addition, the promises you made on your wedding day are the most important, most serious, most self-defining commitments you have ever made. This is why two of the thoughts that constantly bounce through your head are: "*I do not want to fail in this marriage.*" "*What does this say about me as a person if my marriage is over?*"

If those thoughts weren't plaguing you, brother, you would have left her already.

A father third. Kids are great, but they are secondary to the marriage. It simply follows that if one of your roles as a father is to teach your children to grow up and become responsible, complete adults you cannot do that, you cannot be a good father, if the model you present to them as a man and as a husband is not only flawed, but fractured.

You are the example your children learn from. A little girl pushes a toy baby carriage because she wants to be like her mom. A little boy has a toy tool belt and a plastic hammer because he wants to be like his dad. You have seen your children imitate you. It's made you smile.

Now remember this. Every time you yell, you are teaching your children it is appropriate to yell at your spouse. Every time you curse your wife and deride her, you are telling your son, tacitly but unequivocally, that this is the way men treat their dates, their wives and their daughters. Every time you slam a door, every time you shout, you show your kids how adults should behave. They are going to imitate you.

If you want to be a better man, you must set a better example.

If you want to be a better man, you have to stop hurting your children.

HUH? Who's hurting the kids here?.... If you are yelling or acting in an angry manner, throwing things, smashing things, slamming doors, stomping, etc... You are hurting your kids.

Consider this: get a happy puppy. Put the puppy in the center of the room. Yell, scream, and stomp. Notice the puppy has run to a corner. Notice the puppy is trembling in fear. Notice the puppy will try to avoid you. Notice the puppy......

Your kids are just as smart, just as intuitive, just as feeling as the puppy. You may think your anger is between you and your wife, but it's not: it is a family affair and every harsh word, every violent act; every biting sarcasm will find secondary targets, and strike them with the most extraordinary force.

When you say "let's talk about this" you are teaching your children to talk. When you say "I'm sorry" you are teaching your children to accept responsibility. When you treat your spouse with respect and affection, you are teaching your children to have respect and affection for others.

The next time you feel hurt, the next time you feel righteous or victimized, you might think first of your children. Don't trash your side of the street by teaching your children bad relationship skills. Don't trash your side of the street by not respecting the needs of your kids. Don't trash your side of the street by not fulfilling the promise you made when your child was born: to be the best father you could.

Fourth, a Professional. I don't care if you are a garbage man, a lawyer, or a demigod, being a "professional" is crucial to whom you are as a man. If you are inclined to do as little as possible, to sit on your ass, to avoid responsibility in your job, that's probably who you are in your marriage, as a father, and as a man.

If you are a professional you take pride in your work, you teach your children that how you do what you've said you will do speaks volumes of who you are as a person and that there is value in giving 100%. If you take pride in your work, if you set standards and goals, every day is an adventure, every day is a challenge to surpass the day before. If you take pride in your work you come home a happier man more equipped to be the father and husband you want to be.

HOW DID WE END UP TALKING ABOUT KIDS AND GARBAGE MEN? How is this going to save my marriage? The title says it all. It isn't titled "How to save your marriage by being a better Husband." It isn't titled "How to save your marriage by being a better executive." It's titled "How to save your marriage by being a better man."

Being a better man is all inclusive. You can't do just part of it. You have to bring the complete package to the table. Just being a better father won't cut it. Just being a better husband, neighbor, employee, son, brother, or what ever roles you play from day to day and week to week. You have to be better at all of them. Not all at once, but all of them, and as you improve in every area you relationship with your wife will improve.

KATANA

There are two kinds of Samurai swords: Both are beautiful but they are vastly different. If you go on-line you can buy an impressive Samurai sword with a beautiful case and it will look fantastic over the mantel and when you perform your Kill Bill imitations. A good one will run maybe four-hundred dollars.

The second is a Katana made of tamahagane steel and it will set you back three grand for the starter model.

"Samurai sword" is a generic name for any curved sword vaguely associated with feudal Japan and the antics of John Belushi. Most modern swords, including the vast majority of WWII relics, are cold forged from blanks. A blank is something that resembles a sword, but it is thicker, longer, and has no cutting edge. The excess steel is ground off to shape the blade, which is then sharpened and polished, attached to a hilt, matched with a case, and packaged in a land-sea container for sale all around the world. A good factory can spit these swords out faster than you can say "inscrutable." They are very real, very functional swords.

The Katana sword evolved in the Muromachi period, (15th century, give or take). It is made of tamahagane steel. It takes four or five workers about a week to make approximately a ton of steel. The steel is separated by its carbon content. Low carbon steel is used to make the core of the sword, and the skin of the sword is made by "folding" the high carbon tamahagane and even higher carbon nabe-gane steel. Folding consists of heating the metals in a forge, beating them with a hammer into a single piece, then heating that piece again, folding it along its long axis and beating it flat again. The folding process is repeated approximately sixteen times.

Once the core and the skin are welded into one and shaped, the straight blade is tempered by heating the blade to over 1400 degrees Fahrenheit and then quenching it in water. In the process, due to molecular differences, the core contracts more than the skin, and the edge of the blade contracts less than the back, causing the sword to arch along the spine of the blade, creating the graceful curve, or sori, associated with the Katana.

The process of folding and tempering removes impurities from the high carbon steel and allows the blade to be flexible and resilient yet remain capable of retaining an incredibly sharp edge. The process of making a true Katana sword can take a year, with over 1500 man-hours dedicated to each blade.

The average married joe is a four-hundred dollar, mass-produced samurai sword. He looks good, and under optimum conditions will perform well enough, but he will fracture under stress and will time and time again. He hasn't been tempered.

The better man is a Katana sword. Although he has been taken from the fire and beaten flat time after time, each beating has reduced his impurities, each heating has made him more flexible.

You wife is the anvil of growth, you marriage is the forge. It sounds horrible, but it truly is not. No relationship worth having is all wine and roses. Stress is not only normal, but essential to growth.

You have chosen, albeit unconsciously, a mate who will challenge you[21]. If you are a miser, odds are you've married a spendthrift. If you are never given to histrionics, your spouse is most probably emotional. If you have never used blame as a negotiating tool, you've no doubt felt it wielded against you.

Over the course of a successful marriage the spendthrift helps the miser to loosen up, the miser helps the spendthrift to learn economy. In an unsuccessful marriage the lines become rigid, her carefree ways become intolerable and the divorce is blamed on her irresponsible spending. She is the yin to your yang, as are you to her. Together you make a whole, but within that whole you are in a constant state of flux and conflict.

If you are to be a better man, if you are to be a Katana rather than a knock off, you are going to take some hits, you are going to go through some rough times, but each experience is purifying, each makes you more resilient. And just like the Katana, the process takes time, but it is time well spent.

---

[21] This is the basic tenet of Imago, the relationship philosophy that derived from Henrix's body of work. It makes so much sense and explains so many relationships you'd do yourself a great service to look into more closely. You can learn more by Googling "Imago" or heading back to the bookstore and heading to the Hs in the self-help section.

CHAPTER 5

TO BE A BETTER MAN TAKE RESPONSIBILITY

The first step in owning responsibility is to totally lose the idea that your shit doesn't smell just like hers does. Crude, but true. You have done your fair share, both inadvertently and intentionally, consciously and unconsciously, to bring your marriage to the crisis point. If it is your firm and unshakeable contention and core belief that it is all her fault, then for the love of God go hire a lawyer and give this book to someone who gives a damn about himself and his marriage.

If you are willing to admit that you may have unintentionally done just a little to bring about the stagnation and conflict in your relationship, all well and good, but lose the equivocations. Lose the *unintentional*, the *little*, lose the *may*. State your truth: I have contributed to the failure of my marriage. Equivocations are mental "buts" that allow you to blame her rather than own your contribution. The unspoken full sentence is "I may have done this, but she did THAT, with either justified my this, or completely overwhelms it."

Stand up at the plate, brother: You have lied, you have said half truths, you have avoided issues, and that's the good stuff you've been doing. You have been non-supportive and critical. You have shouted in anger. You have punished her with silence. Of course it matters what she has done, but she's not here, the title of the book isn't how to save your marriage by making your wife a better woman. You cannot change your behavior, you cannot make yourself a better man, unless you admit and own your own failings, your own misdeeds.

This isn't intended to berate you or blame you. The smart money says you have been doing the best you can. The bad stuff that happens in your marriage seems to come up of its own accord, and you do try to apologize. You did the best you could with the tools you had. You are going to get some new tools in this book, but you will not be able to use them to their best advantage if you don't recognize the damage you did before you got them.

Thus the proper statement is: I did this and it hurt our relationship. Catalog your missteps and resolve to address them. If you can't immediately list at least five things that you do that are destructive to the relationship, you are either comatose, lying, or a hopeless cause.

One of the things we do to hurt a relationship that might not come immediately to mind is to escape. We work, or we exercise, we read, we focus on a hobby, in a worse case scenario we plug into the television or the internet, anything we can do to avoid contact with the antagonist body-snatcher that had become your spouse. We don't think it's destructive because at some level what we are doing is positive.

It's good to exercise. It's good to work, etc… but as my grandmother used to say, to much sunshine makes a desert, and doing the right thing for the wrong reasons just causes trouble.

Other, more blatant destructive behaviors include passive-aggressive behavior, sarcasm, anger, as well as being disdainful and judgmental.

To be a better man you have to change these behaviors. Once you acknowledge them, you must abandon them. You can no longer hide in the computer room or garage, nor can you resort to criticism, anger and silence. This is not as unpleasant a requirement as you might imagine. Think about it: every time you've hidden in a task, been angry, or cynical or deathly silent you have been miserable. Life doesn't have to be that way, and for the better man, it is not.

Ah, but you say, I might be miserable, but I'm less miserable than I would be, which is why I do it.

I know it seems that way, but with the skills you will, hopefully are, learning in this book you will be able to eliminate the misery you hide from… emotionally you may be hiding from the equivalent of gun wielding terrorist, but I'm giving you phasers, Mr. Spock and all the resources of the Starship Enterprise. Trust me: it will be safe to go outside.

The second step in owning responsibility is to do it in real time. That means fessing up when she tags you, when she catches you out, and especially when you realize you dropped the ball, even if she doesn't.

Most times when we get caught in a lie, or when we find ourselves in the unenviable position of not having done something we should have done, we feel vulnerable. And when we feel vulnerable, we become defensive, and defensiveness leads to anger. Consider this scenario:

Mary has asked you to do something and you have agreed to do it. For fun, we'll say it's counting the coffee beans.

Mary: **Did you count the coffee beans?**

Your first thought is *FUCK*, your second thought is *Find an excuse*, and mixed in is a background feeling of resentment because you feel like she's telling you what to do, and of feeling judged and found inadequate, because in her voice you can hear recrimination, so really what you get from her, what you think she's saying is this,

Mary: *I know you didn't count the coffee beans because you never do anything I ask you to do so I'm going to use this opportunity to try to make you feel guilty, and lord knows I'm going to use this against you in our next argument, and in just a nanosecond I am going to get upset and take it out on you by being put-out and emotional. There goes the day, Bub, so get used to it.*

So, your response is to go on the offensive, construe what you've been doing as more important, offer excuses and justifications

YOU: **I've been doing the taxes, Mary, do you remember the taxes?**

And what Mary hears is this:

YOU: *Counting the coffee beans is unimportant, Mary, and by association neither are you, and as you can hear by the moral superiority in my voice, I have been doing stuff for US, saving OUR HOME from tax liens, plus the sarcasm about the taxes is intended to make you feel stupid.*

MARY: **You never do anything I ask you to. You always have time for exercise, you always have time…...**

And you start thinking, *she's got some nerve saying I never do anything for her, I'm always doing her shit and what thanks do I get? …..* and your righteous indignation builds.

YOU: **Never? NEVER? Didn't I…..."**

Is it any wonder you get into a fight?

But consider if you owned it. If you took responsibility for it, and you said:

YOU: **No, Mary, I didn't, and I apologize because I said I would. I know I let you down and I don't feel good about that.**

And guess what that is? It's called the truth. You do feel a little bad, you did say you would, and you did drop the ball. Remember, her question wasn't "Can you give me excuses for why you haven't counted the beans?" By responding with excuses, you not only told her that either you weren't listening or that her question (her, too) was unimportant, but you also opened the door not just for an argument, but you gave it the power to spin out of control into things that happened, other grievances, as you each seek the moral high ground by calling into question the actions and motivations of the other.

Now here's the beautiful part: She has no come back from the truth. The argument will not start because you've given her nothing to fight about. She might be disappointed, she might be angry, but you're not going to have an argument because you are agreeing with her.

Now here's another beautiful part: she is going to appreciate your honesty. She might still be angry but that's okay. By being honest with her, you will allow her the opportunity to be honest with you. Instead of responding aggressively to your defensiveness, you allow her to perhaps recognize your contribution and you might get:

MARY: **Oh, I didn't realize you were doing the taxes. I'd forgotten all about that. You don't know what a load off my mind it is for you to take care of that. Forget the beans; we'll get to them later.**

But you may not, so after you own it, you either immediately do what you say you were going to do or you ask her how she wants you to fix it. And then you do it.

But here's the kicker. Do you remember the misery you were going to avoid? It didn't show up, and you avoided all the angst and misery of the argument. How cool is that?

One of the reasons your marriage is in trouble is because you have stopped trusting each other. Your failure to count the beans reinforced her idea that she couldn't trust you. Attending to the remedy promptly, indeed always doing what you say you are going to do, rebuilds that trust.

Well what about me? What's she's going to do to rebuild my trust in her? LET GO OF THAT. This is about you, not her. But since you ask, as she learns to trust you again, she will, in turn, become more trustworthy. She won't have the excuse of "he didn't do this, so I don't need to do that." In fact, she'll have a positive thought, "he's been doing this and this and this, I think I'll do that."

But even if she doesn't, you are growing, you are becoming a better man, and if it doesn't bear fruit in this relationship, it will in the next.

GIGO

Long before Pentium processors, George Fuechsel was an IBM 305 RAMAC technician/instructor who taught that a program's results were only as valid as the data they used. Bad data begat bad conclusions. His mnemonic for this syndrome was GIGO: garbage in/ garbage out.

The focus of the lesson was that operators should never totally trust any program's result, they needed to step back and compare it against anticipated results, they had to be able to compare real time effects against the results projected by the program, and to challenge the data when the two were at odds.

The processor that is your conscious brain, your neocortex, relies upon the information gathered through your senses, but filtered by reptilian and mammalian brain. Your computer program works just fine, but if it is relying on bad data, you are going to get bad results.

Stay with me. This is going somewhere.

CHAPTER 6

A BETTER MAN TRAINS HIS DOG

The conventional wisdom in the dog park is this: train your dog or it will train you. This means that if you don't teach your dog to heel and it pulls you by the leash then the dog is training you to stagger along like some stiff armed Night of The Living Dead reject every time you go for a walk. It's a neat trick, and don't think the other dogs don't talk about it. They are in awe that not only do you do the trick, but you don't expect a treat either.

Truth: The dog barks uncontrollably and you shout "shut up!" The dog has taught you to shout when he barks. Stimulus, response.

A corollary to this rule is that once a dog teaches you a trick, the dog will expect you to perform it regularly. Say, eating snacks at the dining table. No matter that you haven't slipped Fido a bit of liver in over a year, Fido still sits there, patiently waiting for you to get back into the groove.

One night I lay in bed, awakened at some ungodly hour by thoughts unbidden and unable to fall back asleep. I tossed and turned until I undertook methods proven to help me return to slumber. I urinated. I took asprin. I drank chocolate milk. None of it worked. I couldn't sleep.

I lay there, trapped in a body that refused to do what I wanted, and it dawned on me… (Almost literally) that some how the dog that was my body had trained me to wake up and worry about shit I couldn't do anything about.

With that epiphany, I began to count to one hundred thousand by thousands to give my brain something to do other than obsess, and I made my body breath in a long breath on the number, and exhale on the thousand.

I got to fifty something and lost my count, so I started back at fifty again, and I never made it to one hundred. Never have. Now when I wake up in the wee hours of the morning I do the same routine. I am retraining the dog that is my brain.

I still wake up, but I don't lay there cursing my affliction of insomnia, I go back to sleep.[22]

Our awareness, our consciousness, is the product of three interlinked biological computers: the reptilian stem, the mammalian brain, and the neocortex.[23]

The reptilian stem is the oldest part of your brain; it's the part of you that is barely sentient. It controls all the autonomic functions of the body, like breathing, heartbeat, body temperature, and has a pretty good sense for danger.

The mammalian brain evolved after we crawled up out of the water and developed as we needed a way to process the new experiences, like sunshine, pleasure, feelings. It is where emotional memories are made, where the distinction between fear and pleasure is made.

The neocortex is the brain which developed as we lay on the beach and began wondering about the stars, it allows us to

---

[22] Most of the time.
[23] The triune brain is a concept of Dr. Paul D. MacLean

process symbolism, language, and logic. The neocortex is where you live, where you appreciate time and beauty.

Now, since the stem came first, almost all the information we process, every sensation you have, passes through the reptilian stem, through the mammalian brain, and into the neocortex.

And as information passes through your old brain, it gets spun.

Your great-odd grandfather stuck his foot in that new fangled thing called fire and it burned, and in a pretty much straight-up reptilian way he pulled it out.

His mammalian brain took that information and created a memory. It associated the stimuli, the heat, the light, the smell, with a memory of pain and just like that your great-odd grandfather knew not to put his foot in the fire again.

His neocortex took the information, associated it with other memories, like forest fires and burnt meat and warmth in the cold, and started to divine good uses for fire: cooking, driving game for hunting, staying warm in the winter, and even use as a weapon.

That's how it works when the computers are all in sync. It's pretty much why our species has walked on the moon while our almost genetic twin, the chimpanzee, is still hoping for the revival of the Tarzan movie franchise.

But when it doesn't work, when the reptilian stem puts too much spin on the info; when the mammalian has too many painful memories, that's when the neocortex stops optimal functioning because it's getting bad information.

In that scenario, your great-odd grandfather never learns about bar-b-cue because every time he sees fire the only signal that makes it through to the neocortex is RUN DANGER PAIN

So here's what happened when I woke up at night: The reptilian stem in my brain received a stimulus. Maybe it was a sound in the night, maybe it was a stray thought, who knows. And it responded with a fight or flight, and dumped cortisone, adrenalin and a bunch of steroids into my body to get me up and alert.

As this information passed through my limbic system, my mammalian brain, a bunch of emotional memories got thrown into the mixture so that by the time it reaches my neocortex my heart is pounding, I'm breathing hard, in a cold sweat, and regardless of the original stimulus, I am convinced something bad is going on. My neocortex is working just fine. I can anticipate problems, see dangers, conceptualize disasters, and I can do it again and again.

Mind you, there is no danger and I've nothing to be alert about but my neocortex is operating at full speed on bad information so it all, seemingly, makes sense. GIGO.

But by consciously regulating my breathing I was essentially overriding the brainstem; by using my neocortex to count I was intentionally disregarding the signals from my mammalian brain, and in the process I was able to relax and return to what I wanted and needed to do: sleep.

So let me spell it out for you. The part of your brain that processes fear and regulates your heart beat and breathing is the reptilian stem and limbic system. That is the dog.

Anytime you are in a situation, most often in an argument with your wife, and you feel your pulse rise, feel emotions coming to the surface, feel that surge of anger, know full well your reptilian stem is overwhelming the conscious you. Know full well that your conscious brain is being fed wrong information.

When this happens the mammalian brain starts evoking past injuries and pains and at best you will remember every slight, you will see patterns that justify your dark conclusions, and you will feel self-righteous. At worst you will become reactive and aggressive and possibly violent.

And it will all, seemingly, make sense. The dog that is your reptilian stem has trained your neocortex to have a high degree of confidence in the validity of the input. The dog says jump, you say how high?

The result is that you become defensive and angry, and your conversation will devolve into a fight. What you need to know is that fighting doesn't work for you. It doesn't get you what you want, which is a good marriage. It is a tool that has never worked for you, yet you resort to it in a way that would make Pavlov nod his head and smile. You have been trained to respond this way.

This has happened before and it will happen again and again until you recognize it and then take positive steps to remedy the situation. First, break the cycle. Pause, take a walk, breath, drink chocolate milk, whatever it takes to stop your reaction, to allow yourself to re-evaluate the input. You do not have to be angry, you do not have to be scared, you do not have to be defensive. You can control it.

Now you say: But she's wrong. She is being mean. She is acting crazy. She is attacking me. I do what I have to do to protect myself, to make myself heard.

Well, sure. That's the logical conclusion based upon the data your neocortex is receiving. But what if that information is flawed? What if, when you see that your wife is angry your lower brain reacts just as your greatest of all grandfather's did when he got burned and is feeding your neocortex the functional equivalent of RUN DANGER PAIN. Her anger, like the fire, has incredible benefits if it is respected[24]. In order to gain those benefits, you must disregard the results of your programming that dictate you react aggressively and defensively, and try something new.

If you don't train the dog, the dog is going to train you.

---

[24] Chapter 16

CHAPTER 7

A BETTER MAN HAS COMPASSION

I don't know if you can do this. I suspect you can do it on the easy things. Someone is hurt: you buy them a drink. You nod your head. You say "I know where you're coming from."

But true compassion means understanding and feeling another's pain and in order to do that, especially within the dynamics of a relationship, you have to let go of the pain, and the hurt, the righteous indignation that blinds you.

An example: Mary has stormed out the door and left, saying you are a complete loser. You are understandably distraught. Your wife has walked out and left you with the kids, she's said and believes bad things about you which are wrong and hurtful. The more you think about it the more your pain turns to outrage. How dare she say that, do that, believe that? She has sorely misused you. You have been hurt. You have the right to be heard around that, the right to demand her apology. You have the right…. for who knows what else, but by far and away, she has done wrong. She has no rights. You are the victim, damn-it. It's up to her to fix things.

And that makes perfect sense, but all the rights in the world are not going to resolve anything. Enforcing them will not get you what you want: a happy marriage. And if she does come back, how are you supposed to accept her after all of your anger and angst over this, how are you going to put the genie back in the bottle?

This is what you need to know. Mary has to be feeling conflicted at best. She is coming home because she wants you and the family. She probably feels guilty about leaving, she probably feels justified in leaving. She's angry with you; she doesn't know how to apologize. She is afraid of your righteous indignation; she doesn't want to admit she was even a little wrong because she fears that you will make her assume responsibility for being totally wrong. She is worried what abandoning the kids says about her as a mother, she feels foolish…. And that's just the stuff that pops up off the top of my head.

Because she feels threatened and scared she will, more than likely, respond to anything you say with either vocal anger or deadly silence.

If you walk around in your morally superior sackcloth and ashes she is going to feel judged and respond defensively. You have to let go of the anger and pain you feel, let go of your righteous indignation. You do this by going back and addressing the fears that precipitated your anger, naming them and then letting it go.

If you begin the conversation with something witty like, "Come to get your clothes?" Or "What have you got to say for yourself? Or even "Are you going to take the kids to soccer?" It's probably not going to go well. Even if you don't say anything, but, because of her guilt she suspects you are walking around in your morally superior sack cloth and ashes, it is not going to go well.

Imagine if, upon her return, you were to try to see the world from her perspective and to say: "I know you must be feeling very confused. I know how important family is to you. I know you must have been under a lot of stress. Clearly there are things we need to talk about, but we can do that after things have settled down. I am glad you are back. I love you."

And every bit of that is the truth, but if you focus on your pain, your need to be right, you are never going to see it, never going to say it, and she is never going to know that you want to and can understand her. That is compassion.

What can she say but "thank you," how can she feel anything but your concern, and in the process maybe she can let go of some of her reactivity so that when the two of you do get around to the talk she is more composed, more rational, as are you.

This isn't to suggest that you don't get to have your say, that you don't get to address the issues, or how her behavior affected you. You are not approving of anything she did, but neither are you judging her.

So what do you do with your righteous indignation? Where do you go to get your propers? *I mean, brother, she did me wrong. I need and deserve an apology. It's all well and good for me to understand her, but who's going to understand me?*

You have a point. But the unspoken tenet of your argument is instant gratification. You want your propers now. The truth is that she can't do that now. Understand, it's hard enough for you to be compassionate towards her, and you know what you're doing and why. How can you imagine that she has the present capacity to let go of her victimization long enough to see your pain? She hasn't got a clue at present, and may never. Period.

Here's the truth. She will never, ever recognize and acknowledge the pain she has given you as long as you demand it of her. It just doesn't work that way. It doesn't work with you, does it? If you shout out your pain and your victimization at her hands you will get exactly what you have always gotten with that tactic: nada, bumptkis, and more of the same.

But if you show compassion, if you are the better man, the best man you can be, there is at the very least a good possibility, and in reality a better than even chance, that she will come to you later and tend to those injuries she so grievously inflicted.

By restraining yourself, by not demanding the immediate recognition of the injustice you suffered, by showing compassion, you free her from her instinctive need to protect herself from your justified indignation by becoming defensive and reactive and she will have the opportunity to revisit her actions and to feel safe enough to engage you in dialogue.

If you lead in this regard, you will get your propers. It will take time, but it will come.

In the meantime, if you need someone to nod their heads in agreement, buy you a beer and to say "How about them Pats?" then tell a friend, but not just what she did, but how it made you feel, too.

The guy had a dog. Flanders was a big dog, an immensely goofy golden: ball centric; vastly energetic. He liked to lead on walks, jump on new friends, and shove a dirty snout into guests' laps to deposit an even dirtier, spit sodden tennis ball.

Flanders barked uncontrollably at the letter carrier. He chased squirrels with a passion that was not tempered by the inherent dangers of busy streets nor inhibited by leashes. The evilly sharp pronged bad-dog choke collar was as effective at controlling him as the fleeting notion of abstinence on a horny teenager.

But it wasn't always like that. When he was a puppy he'd come when called, even joyfully. He had been easy to housetrain and when he became overly rambunctious it was easy to pick him up and put him in his crate. The one he'd destroyed before his second birthday.

At one time everybody had liked, even loved, Flanders, but that fondness had begun to fade when the dog learned he could drag heavy outdoor furniture across the patio to get to the hamburgers on the grill.

So the guy took Flanders to a dog therapist, who hypnotized the golden and implanted suggestions of good dog behavior. It didn't work.

So the guy took Flanders to a dog whisperer, who, after his initial consultation, explained that Flanders had been traumatically scarred in a prior life and that crating him had exacerbated the injury. The whisperer changed the dog's diet and provided an assortment of herbal supplements. It didn't work.

So the guy took Flanders to a dog trainer, who took the dog for a walk around the yard and in no time at all, the wayward beast was heeling, sitting, staying, coming, and lying down, all on command. It seemed a miracle.

The trainer showed the guy how to use a regular choke collar to get Flanders' attention. He told the guy about short, precise commands that the dog could understand. He told the guy that in order for the fix to work, the guy would have to be consistent in his use of commands, in his use of the collar, in his relationship with Flanders. He walked the guy through it all a dozen times, and Flanders acted like the perfect dog.

The guy calls back a week later. It didn't work; it didn't take, Flanders was his old uncontrollable self.

Did you use the simple commands? No, but Flanders knows a lot more than you give him credit for. *Did you use the collar correctly?* No. Flanders wouldn't let me. He pulled constantly. *Were you consistent with Flanders, always enforcing the rules?* Well, no. He likes to lead on his walks, I can't take that from him, and I don't mind if he's on the sofa when I am, it's just when I'm not there that it's a problem.

Okay, the trainer said. *We'll need at least ten sessions, but I'm sure we can get on top of this.*

The guy said he get Flanders after work and be there for their first appointment.

No. Leave Flanders at home. You're the one we need to train.

The guy and Flanders' relationship didn't work because they had gotten into bad habits. They both contributed, but the guy thought it was Flanders' fault, and as long as it was the dog's fault, as long as the dog was incorrigible, the guy wasn't responsible. He was just doing the best he could with a bad situation.

The trainer showed him how it could work, and gave the guy the tools he needed to make it work, but the guy didn't use them. He wasn't consistent, he wasn't committed. He slid back into his old easy habits. He had trouble with his relationship with Flanders, but the problems caused by that trouble were easier to deal with than the pain and discomfort that was came from his attempt to change his way of relating to the dog, to learn new commands, to establish and adhere to new behaviors. It was too much work. It wasn't easy.

Plus, if he didn't have an excuse handy, like the dog loves to lead on a walk, he could always fall back on his core excuse: Flanders is unmanageable. It is Flanders' fault. No one can make the dog behave, and that's just the way it is.

Nothing in your relationship is going to change if you remain the same.

CHAPTER 8

A BETTER MAN LISTENS

I have a friend who plays solitaire on his computer when he is on the phone. When I am talking to him I can tell when he is not listening by the clicks on his keyboard and mouse. He doesn't think I can hear them. It bugs me.

Your wife knows you better than I know my friend, and she knows the tells you think she can't see. Listening is not just being in the room with someone who is talking, and she knows when you're not listening, and just like I'm irritated by my friend's multi-tasking, she justifiably resents it.

In "Oh God[25]," George Burns, in the title role, admits that while he always hears prayers, he doesn't always listen. It's a cute thing to say when you are the omnipotent creator of the universe, but it doesn't work in a marriage of equals. Not listening is tantamount to stating "you are not important." And the corollary to that is "I am more important than you," which is effectively the same as I don't love you.

And sometimes just listening isn't enough, especially if the speaker is used to being ignored. Effective listening requires showing the speaker that she is being heard.

Only about 30% of what we get out of a conversation comes from what the person said. The rest of it comes from body

---

[25] Warner Bros. Pictures, 1977

language, intonation, facial expressions, and a big chuck of it comes from what we think the other person is trying to tell us.

Mary starts off with a sentence, and before she's well begun you are already pretty sure of where she's going and ready to provide a response.

Mary: **I don't know what to do about Jane. Her teacher says she is acting out in class and Jane says her teacher is lying and I don't know who to believe.....**

And you, because you are a guy, respond instantly with a solution to her problem. Done and done. Problem solved, conversation over, what's for dinner?

But here's the problem. It is as if Mary asked you to help her with her tennis serve, and instead of standing on the side and observing, you stand on the base line and swat them back at her feet, saying "nice one... wide... long...."

In actuality, so many of our conversations are like tennis matches: She serves, and you return, anticipating her response you rush the net and put it away. We are not so much communicating as <u>reacting</u> to what the other person says, or more often, what we think the other person said.

Reacting is not listening.

So to listen the better man shuts up and slows down. Seriously. Stop what you are doing, listen to what she says, repeat it back to her, and don't offer solutions. If she wanted solutions she'd come to you and say,

MARY: **Tell me what to do about Jane.**

And in fact, that's what you thought she said, but she didn't. You offered a solution before she even took a second breath, and even if you got it dead on right, even if you offered her the perfect solution to a thorny problem, even if God nodded his head in agreement, in that perfect moment you seemingly told her that whatever it was that was bugging her was, in fact, simple. Essentially you demeaned her intellect by tacitly stating that it was a thorny problem only because she couldn't see what was so clear to you.

But worse, the reality is that you 1) probably didn't get it dead to rights, and 2) you didn't tell her anything she didn't already know. She's not stupid, you know.

She's honored you by coming to you with a problem. Honor her by allowing her the opportunity to express it completely, and offer a solution only if asked.

Most people will agree that advice is worth exactly what you pay for it, unless it is their advice, which is priceless.

Don't fool yourself thinking your advice is better than anyone else's.

CHAPTER 9

A BETTER MAN COMMUNITCATES HIS NEEDS

Most men are reluctant to ask for what they need. Stating a need is equivalent to stating a weakness, it makes us vulnerable and less safe. It makes us uncomfortable and thus we avoid it.

Just saying you have needs seems emasculating. Men don't have needs. We're more than capable of taking care of ourselves. We can always kill a bison for dinner; we don't "need" anything.

And yet, we do. What those needs are is immaterial, however, when compared to the real truth that by admitting those needs we make ourselves vulnerable. It's like giving shears to Delilah, or offering ammunition to the thief with the unloaded gun. Why on earth should we give someone, even a loving spouse, a great big stick to hit us with when we are down?

If you want to know what your needs are, simply look to those things that she does that most anger you. If you are tee'd off that she doesn't respect you, guess what your need is? R-E-S-P-E-C-T[26]: sing it, brother.

If you are angry that she spends too much money, look to your concerns around financial security. If you feel miffed that she pays more attention to the kids than you, affection might be your need.

---

[26] Ottis Redding, 1965

Having said that, here is a good rule of thumb: don't ask for anything unless you are prepared to accept no for an answer, and guess what? The answer is probably going to be no. Accept it with good grace.

If that seems a bit contradictory, it is. Here's the truth: she's not here to meet your needs. Having your needs met by someone else pretty much stopped once you started to walk and dress yourself, and her desire to try to meet your needs faded as the distance between you grew.

Plus note this well: being respected and feeling respected are two different things. In point of fact she may respect you enormously, but she shows it in ways you cannot interpret, so you end up feeling no respect even though it's there.

The problems we have with our wives are the problems we have with the world. Our familial relationship is a microcosm to the macrocosm that is our relationship with our extended family, our business associations, our community, our politics.

This means if you are not feeling respected at home, you are probably not feeling respected by your mother, or your boss, or even your neighbor. This doesn't mean you aren't respected, it just means you don't feel it.

Why do I need to know my needs and communicate my needs if she isn't going to do anything about it?

Go back and read the title of the book. This is about making you a better man, and knowing yourself, knowing your motivations, knowing your weaknesses is an essential part of the process.

If you've ever given or have attended any presentation about presentations the presenters say over and over again, see it, say it, do it, (or write it.) The idea being that in order for an idea to be incorporated into our lives we need to come at it from different perspectives. See it on the board, repeat it out loud, write it down.

In the context of your marriage and your needs "see it" equates to recognizing it in your self, "say it" is the sharing of your insight, and "do it" means addressing your need on a daily basis.

If you share your weakness, your need, your understanding of a flaw with your wife you make it real[27]. You cannot pretend it doesn't exist, and once you cannot pretend it doesn't exist, you can start dealing with it. Additionally, by sharing with your wife your need you are letting her see a part of you that she's never seen before, and in doing so you are quietly testifying that you are changing, that you are evolving, and if she's the woman you married she is going to want to stick around to see where this change is going, how this is going to shake out.

If, for example, you feel she spends too much time with the kids, and you have shared with her your need for affection, then every time that surge of indignation, or hurt, or betrayal comes rushing out of your reptilian stem into your cortex it is going to be met with your sober recognition of its origins, and it is not going to hurt quite so much.

Mind you, your reptilian stem, like the Wizzard of Oz, is going to demand that you pay no attention to the man behind the curtain, but with practice you can.

---

[27] Your wife might not be the best place to start, *see* Epilogue

CHAPTER 10

A BETTER MAN MAKES POSITIVE DECISIONS

Knowing how you make decisions is an important step in making good decisions. Most of us can list half of a dozen reasons why we decided to do a particular thing, but most of those reasons are developed after the fact. They are justifications for our decisions. Often our justifications conflict with our original intent and that internal conflict is not good: it leads to self-doubt and self-loathing.

Consider the man who buys a new sports car. He bought it because he thought it was beautiful, he lusted for the power, for the prestige, for the self-validation. And as reasons go, all of those are top drawer and perfectly acceptable.

When he brings it home his wife gives him the eye and he is not about to admit he bought the car because it made him feel sexy, or for any other intensely personal reason. He doesn't feel safe admitting it to himself, much less her.

Thus, he bought it because he got a great deal, because the bumper to bumper free maintenance would save money in the long run. The rational justifications for why he bought the car are legion. Here's the problem: it's a lie. He knows it's a lie, she knows it's a lie, and the whole issue gets tossed onto the scrap heap of explanations and excuses for why the relationship isn't working.

The first step to making any decision is to be honest with yourself about why you are making the decision. All things being equal, it's okay to buy a car because you think it makes you look sexy. But just like you need to take responsibility for your mistakes, you need to take responsibility for your truths.

If you tell Mary you bought the car because it makes you feel sexy, there is the possibility that she will scoff, but that is her problem. That is her being judgmental and you can live with that until she grows out of it. What she cannot do is argue about it, or put it with the other grievances under lies, and there is also the possibility that she might agree with you.

Plus, when you justify your decision with after-the-fact excuses you are stating to yourself, unequivocally, that your reasons are not good enough.

There are a myriad of decision making paradigms. A friend once showed me his process whereby he listed pros and cons, weighted each, and then used an arcane algorithm to come up with a numerical value that represented the right decision. If I have no other basis for making a choice, my favorite is flipping a coin. There is one very popular paradigm that you probably use on a regular basis and it yields, about ten times out of ten, absolutely horrendous results, and that is FEAR.

Decisions based on fear are inevitably flawed because they are generally based on false assumptions, for nothing is as bad as you fear it will be, and they are flawed because it puts the cart before the horse. A good decision takes you someplace, a bad decision avoids something.

Consider the car; you decided to justify why you bought the car because you were afraid of Mary's response to your true reason. The net result of that decision is an obvious lie that destroys trust.

Think about this for a second, because I will lay dollars to donuts that everyday of your married life, if not two, three or more times a day in your married life, you make a horrendously bad decision based on fear. You decide to avoid your wife's anger, her reproof, her disdain, her scorn, her rejection, whatever. You decide not to discuss an issue with her because she'll get mad.[28] You decide not to ask her to do something because you know she will decline.

You avoid conflict and you dance around issues, and not withstanding it is definitely a *pas de deux*[29], every time you decide to avoid an issue because you do not want to deal with your wife's anger, disapproval and disdain you are undermining the base of your relationship.

If you want to be a better man, you have to choose not to make decisions based on fear.

This is not an easy thing to do. All of our lives we have been taught to make women happy, and failing that not to make them mad. It is entirely beside the point that we cannot make anyone happy and that we are not responsible for another's feelings, this is the edict that has been handed down from generation to generation, and since we cannot make them happy, we go out of our way to avoid making them mad. And it doesn't work for spit. We'll address anger later in the book. It is not a bad thing. But the point here is not to make decisions based on fear.

You will find you make decisions based on fear in other places as well. You decide not to allow your daughter to do this because you fear she will do that or the other thing will happen. You

---

[28] Actually, because you THINK she'll get mad. Chapter 18 addresses projection.

[29] That's French for "a dance for two."

decide not to ask for a raise because you fear being told you're not worth it. You decide not to even make a decision about divorce, because you are afraid of the change any decision will require.

Here is the decision process the better man uses: he decides what he wants and he choose to do those things necessary to obtain that result. If you decide you want to save your marriage, then you do those things necessary to achieve that goal.

Here's a stupid example. You want to go downtown, but you are afraid you'll get mugged. And it's not an unrealistic fear. In this scenario people are dropping like flies.

If you decide not to go downtown, you are caving to your fears. But, you say, going downtown is dangerous, even foolhardy. I'm not being afraid, I am being prudent.

My answer is that you are rationalizing your decision. Tell me you decided not to go because you were afraid, and you get bonus points for honesty, but you're not getting what you want and you will grow to resent it. I suggest prudence is the process of taking those steps necessary to achieve your goal. If your goal is to go downtown, and people are being mugged, then get the skills you need to defend yourself. Take a Karate class, hire a body guard, learn to use The Force, what ever it takes, you do it so that you can go downtown like you want to.

By the same token, in this book you will learn skills that will allow you to embrace your wife's anger[30], to defuse it, to honor it, and in the process, to never fear it again.

---

[30] Chapter 16

I had a friend who promised his wife to help with his daughter's birthday party, but elected to wash his truck instead. When he got home she was angry and he didn't care.

You might be thinking that this is the logical outcome of this decision making process, saying see, he decided he wanted to wash his truck and he took the steps necessary to do it and he didn't worry about his wife's anger.

But here's the thing. He didn't decide to wash his truck. He decided to avoid fulfilling his promise to help with the party. He didn't face his wife's anger, he ignored it. He decided to act as he did because he was afraid of the changes being a better man would require.

A good decision takes you somewhere, a bad decision avoids something. You can highlight that sentence if you want to.

CHAPTER 11

A BETTER MAN TRIES THE JACKET ON

In the course of this process of becoming a better man someone is going to challenge a core assumption you have about yourself[31]. Someone, maybe your wife, is going to say "Have you ever thought that you did this because of Blahblahblah." And that blahblahblah probably doesn't say anything good about you.

Your first reaction, my first reaction, is always going to be "HELL NO. How could you think that? That's not who I am. That's not how I act, that's not what I believe."

And you're going to want to leave it there. Asked and answered. We don't need to bring that up again. Ever.

But a better man embraces challenges to his preconceptions. I liken it to shopping for great used Harris Tweed jacket, and a friend finds one two racks over and tosses it to you. You look at it, you're not sure about the color, and you don't know if it will fit, but you are never going to know if the color suits or if the jacket fits unless you try it on. Unless you pull it up over your shoulders and stand in front of the mirror and give it a good look-see.

If you want to reach your goal to be a better man, you have to try the jacket on. When someone suggests that this behavior is based on fear, or that something else is your main concern, or that your motivation is truly to be found somewhere other than

---

[31] Epilogue

where you suggest, you cannot simply decline to consider it without doing yourself harm.

You have to embrace it. You have to adopt it. You have to let go of your reservations and consider if in fact your friend is right. You have to revisit whatever the issue is and ask yourself: Was Blahblahblah my motivation. Does it make sense that it would see it was my motivation? Can I, in the privacy of my own mind, see any truth in the assertion?

In statistical analysis one doesn't prove a fact, one disproves the alternatives. You don't say: the ball is red. It's red because I know what red is, and bingo, it's red.

You say: I have a premise that the ball is red, but before I can be sure the ball is red I must first entertain the possibility that it is blue, and test for blue, and if I find with mathematical certainty that it is not in fact blue, I must consider if the ball is yellow, etc.

It is the same with yourself. If someone suggests you acted selfishly, it doesn't do to simply say "No, I am generous." Before you can assert you are generous you must consider if you are in fact selfish, and you cannot consider it if you do not embrace it, if you don't try the jacket on.

Here's an example. I was in a counseling session, my partner, Sally, complained about something I had done, and I, being a reasonable person, began listing the neutral and rational reasons that underlay my action. The therapist told me I was being defensive.

My first thought that she didn't understand I was listing **neutral** and **rational** reasons, so I began to repeat myself, and so she repeated herself: I was being defensive.

My second thought was that I was being double-teamed by the two women and getting the old "it's your problem because you have a penis" routine, so feeling a little judged, and thus a little vulnerable and a tad defensive I told her that I wasn't being defensive, I was just *explaining* myself.

And she said, "Exactly."

And I said, somewhat incredulously, "You're saying that by explaining myself I am being defensive?" To which she said, "Yes."

Now that didn't make any sense to me, because I knew, above all else, that I was a sensitive, rational and compassionate guy who was accepting of others and definitely not defensive. That jacket didn't fit. So I shut my mouth and let them talk while I pondered what the hell she was talking about.

I was still pondering when we left, but eventually I gave it a try and tried on the jacket, saying, "Okay, crazy as it sounds, I am defensive when I offer explanations for my actions." It took a couple of days before I realized that my partner had been talking about how she felt about my action, and that my explanation about why I acted as I had was tantamount to saying,

"You are wrong to feel that way because…" and telling her she was wrong was….. *Defensive.*

In other words, she expressed discontent with my actions, I felt, misunderstood and judged by her discontent, which hurt, and my list of reasons why was my defense to that perceived attack.

Sally had been talking about how she felt. If she has said "I was frightened when you jumped in the river to save the child," my *rational* response of "C'mon, Sally, the water was three feet deep, I'm a great swimmer, I had a life vest on, a float for the kid and I was secured by a life line," would be both my honest attempt to assuage those fears and a defense of my action. It would come across as saying "you shouldn't have been scared."

Thus, Sally shared with me that she had been scared when I saved the kid and I responded by saying, in essence, she was wrong to feel that way.

She thinks (correctly) that I didn't understand her and she repeats herself, and I think upon the second iteration of her fear, "What is she saying? That I shouldn't have saved the kid? That I shouldn't do anything that scares her…" and before you know it she's in the bedroom and I'm standing by the lake demanding "What? What did I say?"

Okay. I digressed a bit there. The point is that if I had dismissed the therapist's characterization of my explanations as defensive as being wrong-headed, or stupid, or fem-speak, or just confused, I wouldn't have seen where she was right. I had to consider that I had been defensive; I had to try on the jacket, and guess what? It fit.

CHAPTER 12

A BETTER MAN IS NOT JUDGMENTAL

Imagine this: you are sitting at a red light in the left turn lane, the car in front of you has out-of-state plates, and just as the green arrow illuminates so does the right hand turn indicator on the car.

"What an idiot," you grumble. "Did you get your license on E-bay?" You honk the horn. You throw you hands up in the traditional what-the-fuck gesture. You pound on the steering wheel, and finally, in the last seconds of the yellow arrow, you slam your car into gear, burn rubber as you swerve around the out-of-state loser, laying on the horn just to let him know what a rube he is.

As you speed down the road, another car pulls across the street in front of you, causing you to actually have to take your foot off the accelerator and tap the brakes, and you think "What is it with these people? Is it drive-like-an-idiot day?"

When you stop at the next light, which you would have made but for the two idiots, a heavy set man jogs slowly by and you think, "What a pig."

Judging people is so much fun because by definition, if we are finding fault with them, we must be infinitely superior, and that feels pretty damn good. In point of fact, it feels so good that when you cut through the intersection on the yellow, the other drivers all commented on what an idiot you were, and the guy in the car that crossed before you thought you'd be better served to try to stay within ten miles of the speed limit, and the fat guy took one look at your car and wondered what you were compensating for.

We judge others so often that we forget their humanity. We become so indignant at their obvious incompetence that we don't ever try to see that the fat guy has lost forty pounds in the last year, or that the car that darted across the street had difficult sight lines or that the out-of-state turner was just trying to get to the hospital.

And being judgmental, finding fault in others, makes it so easy to overlook the fact that we were speeding, the honking as you passed the out-of-stater was gratuitous at best, and that while we might not need to lose a few pounds, our dental hygiene isn't what it should be.

Well, maybe so, you say, but there are times when being judgmental is necessary. At work, I have to give employee reviews and I cannot let my daughter leave the house looking like a whore, and truth be known, lots of times people are just plain wrong, stupid and there you have it.

Well, first remember that what works at work doesn't work at home (and it may not work at work, either.) And, second, remember that telling your daughter she looks like a whore is not going to endear you to her. All you have to do is say, "I don't like that outfit."

And, yes, as a rule lots of time people are just plain wrong and stupid, but tell what, bucko, nine times out of ten that rule applies to me and you.

You don't like being judged. You certainly don't like it when you feel your wife has judged you and found you lacking. It makes you feel dissed, demeaned, unwanted and unloved. She feels the same way when you judge her, and just as her judgment of you harms your relationship, your judgment of her does the same. If you want to save your marriage you have to stop harming it by being judgmental.

It's not an easy thing to do. It comes so naturally. First, you must become aware of it. When you condemn the driver in front of you, remind yourself you are being judgmental. When you dismiss someone as being overweight, snap that mental rubber band around your wrist and remember you are being judgmental.

And in the interim, listen to your words. Your habit of being judgmental is going to be hard to break, but you can avoid a lot of damage by stifling the urge to share it with the world, with your wife.

"You look like a whore," is a judgment. "I don't like your outfit," is a statement of your truth. Your daughter says "Why?" And you can say why without casting aspersions on her by saying "I think it shows too much skin" or "I think the skirt is to short." In other words, rather than sharing your conclusion.... You look like a whore....you share your truths.

A judgmental statement to your wife might look like, in the extreme, "You ruined our marriage by being a slut." A non-judgmental statement would be "I am having a hard time coming to grips with your affair."

The key here is to avoid statements that include conclusions about others and that avoid the use of "you" and to focus on your truths in sentences that begin with "I".

But you said at the beginning of the book that if your wife was an abuser you should leave the marriage. How can you ask me to be so judgmental?

You're right. It is judgmental, but it is also factual. Saying your daughter looks like a whore is a judgment based on what you imagine a whore looks like, and has no basis in fact. There are plenty of whores who wear business suits, evening gowns, tea dresses, and look every bit as attractive and pure as Jackie Kennedy. Saying your daughter looks like a whore is a conclusion based upon your feelings that the skirt is too short, that the bodice reveals too much cleavage, or possibly that her ankles can be seen beneath her burka. It is subjective.

Saying your wife is an abuser is a judgment based on events and experiences which can be enumerated, and it is a conclusion necessary to ensuring your safety. It is objective.

Say your wife is a slut is subjective. Saying your wife had an affair is objective. Saying the affair ruined the marriage is subjective and judgmental. Stating that you were unable to forgive her and filed for divorce is objective.

The better man avoids subjective conclusions, and the soon-to-be better man, at the very least, avoids voicing them.

THE TREE

In a park there stand two trees, two oaks. On a pretty spring day they seem majestic and eternal. Green leaves are ruffled by gentle breezes against a blue sky. As spring turns to summer they seem unchanged and even unchangeable, but the gentle insults of fall, the shorter days, the cooler nights, take their toll and the leaves begin to change.

On one tree the leaves color and fall, they leave the limbs bare and grotesque against the white winter skies. On the other the leaves remain, and the bright autumn colors turn brown as they protect the tree from the winter's winds.

In the spring, again, the bare tree leafs green, and rustles gently in the breeze, while the other, with its brittle brown leaves, rattles. Its clotted leaves, fused to the stems, allow no growth.

A child looks up and says, "How sad. That tree is dead. Why didn't it let go of its leaves?"

The moral: let it go. Whatever the insult, the pain, the hurt, let it go. Let those wounded leaves fall to the ground where they can mulch and nurture your roots. Learn what ever lessons you can from your pain and then let it go.

People who hang on to insult the way a dead tree hangs onto leaves are just as dead. Their pain blocks their ability to grow, to seek new insight. You've met these individuals, they are the ones still angry about a divorce that was final ten years earlier, or a business deal from the past, and even those rabidly obsessed with the peccadilloes of past presidents. Just the slightest suggestion brings forth passion, anger and angst as if they were betrayed just that moment.

Hanging on to past hurts does nothing but pollute your life, and make you, on the whole, horrible company and a bore. Let it go.

The most self-empowering words ever spoken are "I forgive you." Whether the forgiveness is for a dead parent's misdeeds, or a lover's betrayal, forgiving that trespass (and I think that's in a prayer somewhere) allows you, the forgiver, to move on.

CHAPTER 13

A BETTER MAN IS NOT A VICTIM

We're not talking about chalk outlines at crime scenes, we're talking about a mind set, a mentality that allows us to blame others for our problems.

Consider this: I met a date's father when I was seated next to him at one of those family pre-Thanksgiving dinners where Uncle Bob takes the congregants out to the cheap restaurant down by the expressway. His first words to me were "Marrying her mother was the worst thing I ever did. She ruined my life…." And he went on, hardly stopping to order, as he laid out the litany of misuse and abuse he had suffered at his ex-wife's hand.

Every problem, from his finances to his health to his troubled relationship with his daughter, he laid at his ex-wife's feet. He was so angry I wondered when the restaurant staff would mop up the vitriol that was pooling around his chair. I was floored, not only by such incredible intimacy from a man I had just met, but by the fact that the divorce was twenty-five years ago: had I not know better, I would have guessed yesterday, tops.

For twenty-five years the man had been living with unfocused rage and an incredible sense of injustice. It clearly consumed his every thought, and that, brother, is one of the biggest problems with being victim: it will consume you.

How do you know if you are a victim? If you use sentences that begin with

It's her fault because…
It's not fair…
Why should I….

And if you are using these sentences long after the event in question.

And you don't have to use these sentences out loud. Just thinking that way is enough.

When we say something isn't fair, we are saying that by some subjective paradigm to which we subscribe but attribute to the world someone else has put us at a disadvantage and that disadvantage should be rectified.

We are making ourselves self-important. We have been misused, and when we are misused, we release ourselves from responsibility: Someone else started it, it is not our fault. When we have been misused, we focus on our own abuse, and not the abuse we deal out, we become blind to ourselves, unable to avail ourselves of introspection because we are busy blaming.

When we say something isn't fair, when we claim the mantle of victim-hood we are the most important people in the world.

And it feels good. It doesn't do us any good, but it feels good enough. Until you think about Uncle Bob's brother and how living with anger, angst and hurt does nothing for you but raise your blood pressure and drive away your friends.

 A better man doesn't use the word "fair" unless it in the context of a carnival.

Even if you wife did do the most unambiguously unfair thing to you, even if come Judgment Day God himself would tell the angels to lay off the hosannas so everyone could hear how she done you wrong and then come down off His throne to commiserate with you, even given that evidence of objective and real unfairness, here's what's wrong with you saying "It's not fair."

First, it let's you focus on her problems, her misdeeds and your misery instead of what's important: you being the best man. It allows you to say I don't have to do this because she did that. Worse, it allows you to justify your withdrawal from the relationship, it allows you to say, "See, she doesn't love me…"

Second: until you let go of "fair" you are stuck in the past, you are wallowing in your misery and self-pity. You are not growing, you are not improving, you are hiding in a corner sucking your thumb and pretending it tastes like strawberries.

Third: who cares? I mean, really, outside of you and God, who cares? I know that's pretty cold, but brother it is true. Nobody can fix it. Unfairness is, by its definition, unfixable, for even if it were remedied, the fact that it happened will always be there.

This isn't to say that if you've been hurt you shouldn't grieve, if you've been misused that you shouldn't get mad or that you should go through life and just take it like a man: stoic and never shedding a tear.

This is to say that you have to get over it. I know that sometimes it may take a while, and that's okay, but you have to let go of it and the sooner the better.

I have a friend, a woman whose family was done an extraordinary disservice by her father. Every time we met it came up in discussion and she talked about it angrily, but every time we talked about it we talked about it less the next time until about two years after the event when it didn't come up again. Her talking about it had been her way of exorcising the pain visited upon her, and the time it took was directly proportional to the intensity of the pain.

A year or so later she brought it up again, this time only to acknowledge that what he had done had hurt her, but hurting her hadn't been his intent, just a foreseeable consequence. Her anger was gone. A year after that she shared that she felt sorry for her father, whose need had been so strong that he had betrayed his family to pursue it.

While she initially dwelt upon the unfairness, she had let it go, refused to be a victim, and thus traveled the natural path from betrayal and anger to forgiveness and compassion.

Compare that to Uncle Bob's brother.

I am not a big fan of fair. I've never seen it anywhere. When the wolf is running down the deer, the deer is focused on survival, not fair. If the deer is focused on fair and bemoaning his fate before the forestland denizens, screaming: "This isn't fair. I was just eating grass. I've never done anything to offend the wolves", then the deer is dinner.

And from the wolf's perspective, he's hungry and he's going about the business of getting dinner from the plentiful bounty his creator provided. He's not thinking about "fair," and if he did he'd think it eminently fair: he's got a family to feed.

"Fair" is always subjective. Your fair is always someone else's unfair.

What is important for the better man is not how others treat us, but how we treat others. When you get to heaven St. Peter is not going to ask you about how tough it was for you, but how tough you made it for others.

The siren call of victimization lures us, compelling us to draw nearer so that we might wrack the ship that is our life on the unseen reefs and shoals of self-pity.

Being a victim is a very powerful thing. When you are a victim, you are the most important person in the room. When you are a victim, you are the one who has been done wrong by the world, you are the one who deserves redress, you are the one that merits sympathy and even respect for the miscarriages you have endured.

Anytime you feel the urge to say "It's not fair…" that I have to do the hard work, that I have to listen, that I have to mirror, you are attempting to absolve yourself of responsibility. You need to stop right there and own it, then let go of it.

You cannot be a better man and a victim.

CHAPTER 14

A BETTER MAN DOES WHAT HE WANTS TO DO

This does not mean that a better man goes to see a movie rather than count the beans like he agreed to do.

This does not mean that a better man sets his interest above all others and he moves through his life like a battleship simply ignoring what he doesn't destroy.

This means that a better man knows what he wants to do, and does it.

Ask a lot of men what they want to do and more than half will offer you an escape fantasy. I want to build a house in Montana and bottle raw honey. I want to sail around the world. I want to chuck everything in my life and go somewhere else. An escape fantasy is all well and good, but it isn't so much a statement of what you want to do as what you want to avoid, which is generally the inexorable grind of day-to-day life in a complicated world that requires constant interaction and didn't come with a rule book.

Very few will say "I want to work forty, maybe fifty hours a week so that I can just barely meet the families expenses, do laundry in the evening and struggle with a life of quiet desperation," even though that is what they are doing day-in and day-out.

But a better man, when asked what he wants to do with his life, will tell you in no uncertain terms what that is, how he is going to reach it while meeting the obligations[32] he has already assumed, and where he is in the process.

For some men, it might be an Iron man competition, a pilot's license, or hitting the high-notes on a clarinet with a number 5 shingle on the mouthpiece. Some might find their goal in their church, or even in their business. Other's might find it in painting or sculpture… some might even write a book or learn to surf.

The thing is that somewhere deep inside of you is something you have always wanted to do and haven't done, a goal you dreamed of but set aside. The fact that it still lingers in your consciousness is testament to how important and powerful that goal is. Nine times out of ten, when you think about not attaining it, you feel a tinge of regret, of self-judgment, or perhaps of despair. You cannot be a better man without pursuing your dreams.

You need to reach that goal, and you need to do it in a way that is respectful of the other responsibilities you have assumed over the years. If you are a surgeon and a father, you cannot simply join the Peace Corps, no matter how powerful the lure. You have responsibilities to your family, your patients and your partners.

You can, however, share your dream with your spouse and your children, you can become involved with the project in ways that do not require immunization and sleeping with bugs. When you share your dreams you share yourself, you give those you love an insight into the incredible person you are, and when you take positive steps to attain that goal while being true to your commitments, you will inspire their respect and admiration, but more importantly you will be doing what you want.

---

[32] Meet your commitments seriatim. *See* Chapter 4

Perhaps there will be an overseas deployment with the Peace Corps after your kids have graduated college. Your wife might join you or she might simply encourage you. Perhaps your drive to serve will be met more close to home with a Habitat for Humanity project.

If your dream is stand-up comedy or even growing the largest pumpkin in the state, setting aside time to reach that goal, and striding methodically towards it, will help balance your life and make you a better man.

And it may be that your goal, this dream that has been in your head since your youth, is to be the CEO of a Fortune 500 company. All well and good as long as you share the dream and you attain it in a way that is respectful of your other commitments: man; husband; father; professional.

Okay, so you just finished the paragraph above and you're thinking "*Jeezo-pete, what a load of happy crappy. Of all the things I have to do, taking voice lessons just doesn't cut the mustard, no matter how much I want to sing the role of Monterone in Rigoletto*"

And that's where you are dead wrong. Go back to the front of the book and start reading again. It says somewhere that it is not enough just to be to the best husband or the best dad, but that you have to be the best man, the complete package, and you cannot be the complete package if you are not taking care of yourself.

Write this down: You cannot be the best man you can be, you cannot be the best husband or the best father if you are not happy. Happy counts. Happy so often gets swept up with the other detritus of our chaotic lives. We forget, or become disinclined, or think we don't deserve to be happy.

From a father point of view, do you want your kids to grow up to be miserable? Unhappy? Well don't forget you are setting the example, and if you wander around the house functional but fundamentally unhappy you are teaching them that this is what they should expect to experience as an adult.

But more importantly, if you are going to be the bring the complete package to the table, if you want your wife to love you as she once did, if you want to bring the joy back into your life, happiness is essential.

You have to nurture yourself, you have to reward yourself, and you have to take care of yourself if you expect to come to the table prepared to be the best man you can be. I'm not saying that you're going to be all sunshine and joy, a veritable Paul E. Anna, but if you are ever going to be truly happy, you need to get your foot in the door, you need to get started and get into practice and that means identifying what you want to do and taking concrete steps towards achieving it.

And remember this: happiness is contagious. If you share with your family your operatic goal, when you attain it they will be almost as ecstatic as you when you take your bow, and by your example they will be inspired to define, share and reach their own goals.

CHAPTER 15

A BETTER MAN CONTROLS ANGER

My friend Sulaiman said "when you take control, you lose control." He meant that when, in the midst of an argument, you decide enough is enough and really let lose you have lost all control over yourself, you are letting the little boy run rampant, you are letting the reptilian stem of your brain control your intellect[33].

Here is a tool: behind every anger there is fear. Anger is a defense mechanism we use to protect ourselves when we are afraid. When you get angry, if you think about it, you first felt threatened. Perhaps she said something that you feel insecure about. Perhaps she pointed out where you were obviously wrong. Perhaps you felt judged, or misused, but whatever it was, you felt afraid. If you can find that fear and acknowledge it the anger will go away. It's that simple.

Conversely, when you are talking to Mary, if you can help her identify her fear, her anger will go away too. Notice I didn't say if you can identify her fears, but if you can help her identify her fears. There's a big difference. When you identify her fears you are, of necessity, judging her[34]. When you help her, you are being supportive and allowing her to judge herself. There will be more about this later.[35]

---

[33] Chapter 6
[34] Chapter 12
[35] Chapter 17

But back to you, here's an example, in the course of a conversation turned to argument over money, Mary says something to the extent that if you earned more money the issue would not be an issue, and you get angry. By her words and her tone Mary has judged you and found you lacking. You don't make enough money. Perhaps you feel her disdain, or rather your shame, and having it pointed out hurts, or maybe you think you make more than enough and that Mary is being unreasonable, in which case you feel unappreciated, and a bit of the martyr.

If you think about it, when you get angry you can feel it come on. It swells in your head like a tsunami, you can feel the waters retreat from the shore as they are sucked into the massive wave that will inundate and overwhelm everything.

And it feels good. It's supposed to feel good. It is a survival skill. It allowed your ancestors who'd finally learned not to burn their feet to counter any perceived threat. Unfortunately, atavistic survival skills are not the best tools for relationship maintenance. Plus, no matter how good it feels in the instant, at best it only postpones problems, it resolves nothing, and only serves to raise your blood pressure, flood your system with corrosive steroids and generally shorten, not just your marriage, but your life.

To get a handle on your anger, to control it, you must first recognize it, and once you recognize it, you must step back. It's called the Pause. You feel the anger coming, and you say to yourself: nothing good will come of this. I will blow up, and she will retaliate. We'll both say regrettable things and bad will go to worst. I've been there before and it doesn't work.

When you pause, you can say: "**Mary, I am becoming reactive. I'm going need time alone. We need to talk about**

this, and we will talk about it, but I need to table it for the moment."

But of course you're not going to do that first time out of the box. It's going to take a fair amount of practice.

The first time you're going to feel the anger coming on, and you are going to roll with it, and when you regret it (and you always do) you'll remember you saw it coming.

The second time, maybe you'll do the same, or maybe you'll just turn and walk out of the room, maybe out of the house. Later, when you've calmed down, you'll come back and say something like: **"I'm sorry I left. I was becoming reactive, and I didn't want to put you through that. I didn't want to do that to us."** And she will appreciate you more than you can imagine.

Still later, as you are calming down you are going to reflect on the origins of your anger, you will identify the fear, and you will be stunned at how quickly your anger has dissipated.[36]

And eventually you'll be able to do it on the fly, feeling the onset, identifying the root, feeling it wash away and moving on into constructive dialogue. I've seen it happen. I've done it. You can too.

To become a better man and save your marriage you are going to become less reactive. You are going to see your anger and fears as they arise and conduct yourself differently. You are not going to let your fear and your anger control your life. You are not going to let your fear and your anger influence the decisions you make. You are going to be a compassionate leader, you are going to be honest about your faults and take responsibility for

---

[36] Truth. It's that simple, it's that hard.

the negative consequences they engender. You are not going to be perfect, but you are going to be better.

Here's a thought for you: anger represents the fear that we will not be heard, that the issue, the hurt we feel must be addressed now and in no uncertain terms. You raise your voice and become aggressive so that you will be heard and heeded instanter.

Once you become confident that you have the tools to be heard and respected, once you are confident that you will be heard when you are ready to address the issue, then the immediate need to be heard lessens and the anger rises less frequently, and then so weakly that it is easily managed..

Red Dog Seven[37]

Here's the scenario: it's second and ten, you are the All American, Heisman Trophy contender, star running back, and as the team huddles a substitution runs to the field with a new play from the coach. He bends into the huddle and calls the play: red dog seven, salad fork on three. The quarterback repeats it and before you can say boo everyone has clapped hands and headed for the line of scrimmage. The problem is you have no idea what 'red dog seven salad fork on three' means. Not a clue: and you know every play in the book. The snap is maybe on three, but that's about all you've got because your team's system of plays doesn't include colors, animals or flatware.

Down.

Set.

Hut... Hut... Hut!

Everybody goes. The quarterback fakes a pump, turns to hand off and gets blindsided by a defensive linebacker, down for a loss of seven, and you haven't lifted a foot.

Third and seventeen: you get some harsh looks in the huddle.

---

[37] the required football analogy

The play comes in from the bench. Red dog seven, salad fork on three. Same play but before you can get your mouthpiece out to say "What the fuck?" everybody is headed to the line.

This time you move on the snap and make a bee-line fore the linebacker. You connect beautifully, setting him nicely on his ass with the unexpected and painful help of the fullback who plowed into your spine, but it's still a broken play and the quarterback scrambles for three yards.

Fourth and fourteen, and you're thinking the punt team is coming on which will give you a chance to ask the offensive coordinator just what 'red dog seven, salad fork on three" means in English, but the specialty team is still holding their helmets at the sideline and the play comes in from the bench: Red dog seven, salad fork on three. Everybody claps and at the beginning of the call you've figured to let the fullback block the linebacker, so at the snap you tuck in behind him, the quarterback fakes a pump, and slams the ball into your stomach but you're not ready for it. You both fall on the fumble and he recovers it for a loss of three.

You get off your ass and you're not looking forward to the conversations that are to come while the defense has the field but as you head to the sideline you notice the down marker on the chains has been clicked over to Five, and your team is back in the huddle.

Fifth and seventeen. Apparently someone has been changing the rules. You don't have to listen to the call to know it: red dog seven, salad fork on three.

This time your arms cradle the ball, you step nimbly around the linebacker who's been flattened by your fullback and you find yourself with nothing but hash marks between you and the goal line. This part you know. Touchdown.

You still have no idea what Red dog seven, salad fork on three means, but it's four to nothing and that's not all bad.

The opposing team kicks off and you're thinking: this is the weirdest game ever. You head out with the rest of the offense to take the ball on the fifty-three when the coach stops you with a hand to your shoulder pad and yells into your ear:

Green cow four, bread knife on two.

And you think: I'm gonna wake up soon.

My friend Daniel found himself in the middle of a bad argument with his wife as he was trying to brush his teeth. It seemed to come out of nowhere; he thought it was unwarranted; he was hurt, affronted and he became reactive. He got angry. He gave as good as he got. Harsh words and Colgate-spit flew and stuck.

Afterwards, as he was reconstructing it, he gave himself a fair amount of grief, saying that he should have handled it better; that he should have been able to embrace her anger; that he should have been able to use the tools he'd learned at The Clearing.

This is the way life is: lots of times nothing makes sense. When you think you know the rules, they get changed. You get asked to do the same thing over and over again, but you are never told how to do it. Success often seems hit or miss, but it comes from keeping your eyes open, paying attention to the fundamentals, and changing to meet the challenges ahead.

The key is to focus on the fundamentals, especially when you don't know what the fuck is going on, when all the rules have been thrown out the window: In the parable, focusing on the fundamentals means being in the right place, coming set, listening to the count, no false starts, paying attention to what's going, and most importantly always coming back to the huddle and returning to the line.

In your relationship and in life it means use the tools you have: pausing, embracing anger, listening, mirroring, being honest with yourself, but most importantly always coming back to repair the damage, always recommitting to the relationship.

Situations happen and there are times you are going to blow it, but know that for the better man failure is essential to success, and your response will improve each time you hear Red dog seven, salad fork on three.

CHAPTER 16

A BETTER MAN EMBRACES HER ANGER

Nothing is more destructive than anger. Nine times out of ten, when she gets angry at you, you immediately become defensive. You find justifications for the action, whatever it was, which sparked her ire. In short order you yell back, you attack by pointing out that her flaws are just as bad, if not worse, than yours.

Here is a tool: acknowledge her anger.

You: **Mary, I can tell you are angry. You are important to me and I want to understand why. Please tell me what is going on.**

Anger is an invitation to dialogue.

This may be the craziest thing you've ever heard, but it is true. When your wife comes at you spitting mad, eye's blazing, body language aggressive and shouting she is offering you an extraordinary opportunity to better understand who she is, to better appreciate her outstanding qualities, to more completely love her.

NO, you say, she's mad; she's totally insane, unreasoning, mean, aggressive, sarcastic, and dangerous. I have two options: Run or give as good as I get.[38]

---

[38] Flight or Fight, remember Chapter 6?

To which I respond: and how is that working out for you? Having a lot of success with that strategy? One of the themes of this book is that what you've been doing hasn't been working, otherwise you wouldn't be where you are.

One of the things you've been doing is assuming that her anger is dangerous. That it is something to be corralled, something to be tamed, that if you let her have at it she will get worse.

In point of fact, you are confusing her anger with your own. You are judging her by your experiences with yourself. And for you it is essential to control your anger, because you're the only one who can do it. But you cannot control her anger. You cannot corral it or tame it. You can't shout it down, you can't beat it back.

Nor do you have to run from it, ignore it or capitulate to it. You simply acknowledge it.

Remember her anger comes from fear. If you understand her fear you will be closer to her. Her anger comes from a sense of injustice. If you understand the values that frame her reality[39], you will better appreciate the incredible woman she is.

Consider this scenario: Mary launches an all out assault. Everything you've done before will lead to a fight. Even abject apologies will not soothe her. Since nothing will work, you have nothing to lose by trying this.

YOU: **Mary, I can tell you're very angry. I love you and it is important for me to understand what's going on. Will you please tell me what happening with you right now?**

---

[39] Chapter 19

MARY: **You know what's going on.**

YOU: **I don't know. I may have an idea, but too often I misinterpret things and my ideas of what's happening with you are wrong. I want to get it right, so I need you to tell me.**

MARY: **I'm mad because when we……**

Then mirror.[40] Be prepared to get an earful. She hasn't got your skill set. You will hear a lot of judgment and blame, but ride with it and don't react. Listen. Mirror. You will learn more about your wife in five minutes than you have in the past five years.

Plus, as she realizes she is being heard, her anger will dissipate. And as her anger dissipates, and as she hears the words she is saying, she will have the opportunity to analyze her thought processes and assumptions. She will have the opportunity, in time, to re-evaluate the blame and judgment that have been the cornerstones of her anger.

And she will see you in a different light, because you've never done this before, and she will appreciate you. Imagine the possibilities attendant to the ability to convert anger to appreciation, and then try to tell me your marriage can not get better.

---

[40] Mirroring is covered in Chapter 17

CHAPTER 17

A BETTER MAN MIRRORS

The frame work for all of this is mirroring. Some call it active listening. Get any of Harville's books and read it thoroughly. The point of mirroring is that 99% of the time when you are having a conversation, you aren't.[41] The other person is talking, and you're getting part of what she's saying, but you are interpreting it based upon your past experiences with her, her body language, her tone, and giving it a nice spin based upon the fears you have and the lies you tell yourself.

You are reacting to her, not communicating with her. You are back on Center Court at Wimbledon, returning as good as you get, anticipating her moves, and hoping to rush to the net to put it away.

Consider Mary says,

MARY: **I saw your mother today…**

Now you know that your mother and Mary don't get along and their fights drive you crazy. Plus, your mother has said mean things and you suspect Mary blames you for not supporting her, but it's all so complicated. Add to that, Mary's got that tone of voice that tells you that she's about to lay a bombshell on you, and of course she brings this up the second you get home, before you've even had a chance to catch a deep breath, so you say:

---

[41] Remember the tennis analogy from Chapter 8

YOU: **Oh, God! Can't you give me a break here? I just got home. What did you say to her? Haven't I told you just to turn the other cheek? She's old, she can't help herself...**

Mind you, Mary hasn't said a word. This is all coming out of your head. You think she's disrespecting you by not giving you time to relax. You blame Mary for not dealing with your mother as well as you.[42] And you are assuming, maybe rightly, that she's about to lay a bombshell on you, so you strike preemptively.

And Mary hears your anger, and she's feeling a little righteous indignation because you interrupted and didn't let her finish, and that's one of your characteristics about you that drives her crazy, especially when you are right. So she lashes back,

MARY: **I didn't say anything to the old bitch, asshole, I was just...**

YOU: **Did you just call my mother a bitch?**

And so it goes. The point I'm making is that whatever else you guys are doing, you are not communicating. You are reacting to each other, and sometimes to your own assumptions. Mirroring will solve this. Guaranteed.

Before I get into the process, I have to tell you it's going to feel awkward, uncomfortable, stupid and graceless. You are going to feel idiotic.

I imagine that is exactly how Tiger Woods felt when he tried out his new swing in public for the first time[43]. Everything thing in

---

[42] As if you got along perfectly with your mother...
[43] Circa 2000

his incredible past, all of his accomplishments, his pride and his muscle memory all said: what the fuck are you doing? And it took practice, but eventually he walked out onto the tee and let his new swing rip and it looked like a work of art, the most beautiful, fluid, ergonomic and efficient swing ever. It looked like he'd been doing it all his life, and incredibly enough, it looked easy.

And although it looked easy, I imagine it didn't seem so to Tiger. I imagine he was thinking very hard about every facet of his swing, and no matter how long he plays golf, his old swing, the one he grew up with, is going to feel more natural, more fluid. And when Tiger gets tired, when the pressure is on, if he loses his concentration he will slide back into parts of his old swing, and as he watches his ball hook or slice, he will revisit his swing and recognize where he backslid, and resolve to hit the ball better next time.

Just so, you have a way of communicating, and it's got good as well as bad points. It seems very natural to you, but it's not working. How do we know this? You bought this book[44].

So you are going to learn a new way to listen, to communicate, and it will feel odd, but if you practice, if you pay attention to your mistakes and resolve to correct them, you will improve.

So go hydrate and do anything you need to do before we start so that you can give this process your undivided attention. When you are ready, sit back, turn on the video camera, get ready to take notes, and…..

Ready?

---

[44] If you're still standing in the bookstore freeloading it is time to buy the book and go home.

Repeat what she says to you.

It's a little more complicated than that, and there are some bells and whistles that can be added, but in essence, the way to save your marriage, if you are committed to being a better man, is to repeat everything she says to you. Verbatim. Word for word.

No, not everything, not "do you want more chicken" or "pass the salt" or "I think I'm going to puke." But the important stuff. The talks. The arguments.

It goes like this:

Mary: **I am so upset with my mother I think I could scream.**

Typically your response might be: "It is what it is" Or "Who wouldn't?" or "What did she do now?" These are all responsive answers, and they can be misinterpreted. She can apply any subtext or connotation, she can even think: He's saying that, but he means this, and then get mad at you for what she thinks you mean even though 1) you didn't say it and 2) you don't mean it.

In mirroring you say,

YOU: **What I'm hearing you say is that you are so upset with your mother you could scream. Is that right?**

And she'll look at you like you dropped off the face of the moon because you've never done that before. So you'll probably have to repeat yourself, "What I'm.... Is that right?"

And she'll say,

MARY: **Yes.**

And you'll say,

YOU: **Is there more?**

And she'll say,

MARY: **It all started this morning when she called and I was getting the kids ready for school.**

YOU: **Let me see if I got this. It all started this morning when she called and you were getting the kids ready for school. Is that right?**

MARY: **Yes, but what are you doing? Why are you repeating everything I say?**

YOU: **I want to make sure I understand you. What you are saying is important, and I have noticed that sometimes I don't listen as well as I should so I'm trying to be a better listener. I know it's awkward, but let me see if it helps. You said "it all started this morning when she called and you were getting the kids ready for school." Then what happened?**

Make sure you repeat her exactly, and make sure you don't get your mouth too full. If she gets too much out at one time you will not be able to mirror it. You can say, "I hate to interrupt, but I want to make sure I heard you. You said…."

Now, if this was all you did, you would see an improvement, because for the first time she is going to feel like you are not only hearing her, not only listening to her, but getting it. Think about your own experience. You like it when people listen to you, even more so when they get your point. She will too.

But wait, just like the late Billy Mays said, there's more. There is a very good chance that she is not upset with her mother, but that she is reacting to her mother because she is upset about something else. By repeating her words to her, your wife gets to hear what she's saying. When you ask "Is there more?" she has the opportunity to amend, or append, to what she has said. You are helping her think through her problem, and that is a good thing.[45]

"It's not just about the phone call..." she may say, or "She always makes me feel like I'm not being a good mother."

Eventually she will come to a natural conclusion. You'll say,

YOU: **Is there more?**

MARY: **No.**

Hah! You're done.

Not yet.

You summarize what she has said. You take a deep breath and say,

YOU: **Let me see if I got this. Your mom's phone call upset you ……… ."** Is that right?
If you've been paying attention, she says "Yes" and you say

HAH! Done!"

Not yet.

_____

[45] Chapter 15

112

You validate the emotions and feelings she has shared with you.

YOU: I can see how your mother's call would make you angry....

Mind you, validation doesn't mean agreeing, and she will not take it as you agreeing with her. It just means that you can see that it makes perfect sense for your wife to feel the way she does. Not from your perspective, but from her perspective. And her perspective includes all her prejudices, assumptions, projections, fears and angers.[46] In time, she may come to adjust the basis for her feelings, she may come to a point where she can re-evaluate her projections, and conquer her fears, but she is not going to do it immediately, and she's definitely not going to do it because you point them out to her.

Saying "You wouldn't feel that way if you weren't convinced your mother was going to lie to you," is essentially saying "you are wrong to feel the way you do because you are wrong about your mother and I am here to let you know that you are wrong." This is the sort of sentiment that can lead to arguments.

So no judging is allowed in validation. It's not approval, it's not educational, it is nothing but saying "Of course you feel that way. It makes perfect sense." And now you say,

HAH! Done!

---

[46] Remember Chapter 6 talks about GIGO and the way everything she's thinking makes perfect logical sense. You can't solve the GIGO problem by telling her she's acting on bad data, you just validate the reality she's experiencing.

Not quite. One more thing: Empathize. Your wife has related a story to you that has strong emotional undertones. She may be feeling angry still, she may be feeling sad that her relationship with her mother isn't what it should be, she may be feeling guilty, she may be feeling relieved. If you listened to her, you should have a guess about how she's feeling, so you say:

YOU: **I imagine you're feeling** _____[47] **now.**

And she says

MARY: **Yes.**

And maybe she says thank you for listening, maybe she says nothing and you say,

YOU: **Thank you for letting me mirror you**. And then you say.

HAH! DONE!

And you are for the moment, but brother, you are just beginning.

There are refinements; there are bells and whistles.

You can use mirroring to engage your wife in a conversation. You say,

YOU: **Mary, I'd like to share something with you if you have the time,** and when she says yes, you say**, I need you to mirror this.** And you tell her what is on your mind in short declarative sentences.

---

[47] Appendix A

114

Piece of cake? Maybe.

First, don't use blame. Keep everything from your perspective. You can assert factual issues, "When you yelled at me." Or "when you shot the policeman" but they have to be followed up with "I felt...." Or "It reminded me of ...."

You don't say "When you insulted Mother Theresa" because there is an implied judgment in that statement that she did something wrong. You say, "When you called Mother Theresa a skanky bitch..." (If in fact she did.) A statement of fact is not judgmental. Then follow up with how you feel about it.

You don't say "you pissed me off today" you say "I became angry when..." the former places blame and responsibility on her, the latter is you owning your own feelings. But you say, *Brother, SHE DID PISS ME OFF. HER BEHAVIOR WAS ATTROCIOUS. I LOVE MOTHER THERESA.* All well and good. Enjoy the argument, because Mary will resent your judgment and find a way to either justify her behavior or counter attack to avoid responsibility for it.

She'll escalate and say "She's not a saint, she's a horrid...." Or she'll say "I didn't start it, The Saint called me a slut." Or, "Where do you get off..." or she'll say "You always take up for the Nuns. Every time, just like the time when you...." And soon you'll be arguing about something else that happened six years ago.[48]

It has happened time and time again. You cannot deny that. More importantly, you cannot continue to do the same thing over and over again and expect different results. The

---

[48] We covered this in the introduction.

communication skills you have been practicing over the years, what ever their merits, are not serving you well. You keep getting into the same arguments. You keep getting emotional. You keep getting hurt and hurting in kind.

Mirroring can also help you avoid the digressions that cause so many hard discussions spin out of control into arguments.

Consider that you are in an intense, intentional dialogue about the coffee beans. You can feel the tension and so can she and somewhere along the way she pops up with,

MARY: **This is just like Mother Theresa all over again! I can't believe you took her side in 1997…**

Now typically, your first reaction is *"Where did that come from?"* Your second is *"I thought that was settled."* And your third is *"How many more times do I have to hear about this?"* and your response is generally argumentative and combative.

YOU: **This has nothing to do with Theresa, and you know it.** To make the point clearer you raise your voice, intending to, if not prevail, at least hold your ground on this issue.[49]

Which tells her that you think she's wrong to bring it up, that you expect her to retreat from the point (like that's going to happen) and that you are ready to escalate the conversation into a fight. A fight you have had so many times before.

But, Jeezpo-pete, what am I supposed to do?

First off, realize that she is redirecting the conversation to a place where she feels she has a moral high ground because she is

---

[49] And suddenly you're not talking about coffee beans any more.

intimidated and frightened. Whether you think she has any cause to be intimidated and frightened is entirely immaterial, it is her reality. And understand she may not be intimidated and frightened by you. It could be that the conversation is taking her places she doesn't want to go. It is a defensive mechanism and she may not even realize that she's doing it, but she's doing it because it has always worked before. The fight she can deal with, the other stuff... she doesn't even want to go there.

Second off, realize that she is bringing it up because it is still in her mind, it still bugs her. You may have mastered the art of letting things go, but she hasn't and she isn't going to learn how to let things go by the expedient of your anger.[50]

So you say, calmly and with sincerity,

YOU: **I can tell you're still upset about Theresa, and that make sense to me. We need to discuss it more and I promise you we'll come back to it, but right now we are talking about the coffee beans...**

By repeating what she said about Theresa, validating it, and empathizing with her all in one sentence you have used a micro-burst of mirroring to let her know that she's been heard and that her thoughts on the matter are important and will be revisited, plus you have de-escalated the conversation by responding to the Theresa issue calmly and with compassion, which is probably something you have never done before.

You have changed the timber and the tone of your discussion and you have prevented a repeat of an argument. If Mary is

---

[50] Remember the story in Chapter 13. There is a natural process for letting go. It takes different times for different individuals, but rest assured that mirroring accelerates the process.

frightened and intimidated by you, then you have shown her that the new and better you doesn't want to frighten and intimidate her, and if she is frightened and intimidated by where the conversation is going, you have gently kept her on track so that together you can explore where her fears will not let her go.

Of course, it is all for naught if you do not return to her soon after the present conversation and say,

YOU: **Mary, in our conversation about the beans you brought up Mother Theresa, and I said we'd get back to it and I am ready, if you are, to hear what you have to say.**

By doing what you said you would do you are rebuilding her trust in you, and you are laying the foundations for better communications because she will come to understand that you are interested in her concerns, and that this mirroring thing has some benefits, in that you came to her to hear those concerns.

Mirroring is a new and awkward skill, but it will change your life. It is difficult and it takes practice. I have given just a sketch of the process and to truly make it work you need to get one of Harville Hendrix's books, see an Imago trained counselor or go to a weekend couples retreat. I get no dime for saying that. I did it. It works. I share it with you.

Mirroring fundamentals
1) repeat what she said; a) ask if you got it right; b) ask if there is more; c) repeat as necessary.
2) summarize what she said; a) ask if you got it right; b) amend as needed.
3) validate what she said.
4) empathize with how she must feel

JOHN PHILLIP SOUSA

"So here's the scenario. These are the facts: across the street is a community center; there is a walkway that leads from the front door to the sidewalk. When you look up you notice a man is carrying a white sousaphone up the walkway to the door..."

"What's a sousaphone?" John asked.

"It's like a tuba, but with the bell turned forward, to bring the sound forward. It was designed by John Phillip Sousa. That's not the point. The point is that it's so big that you immediately notice it, and the guy carrying it, and you wonder, "What the hell is he doing?"

"So what was he doing?" Ken asked.

"I don't know."

"Who is John Phillip Sousa?" John persisted, clearly not with the program.

"He was the leader of the Marine Corp Band. He wrote 'Stars and Stripes Forever.' Again: not the point."

"So what was the guy with the horn doing?" Larry followed up Ken's query.

"I don't know. You tell me."

"How the hell should I know?" Larry dismissed the issue.

"Well, guess. Make something up."

"Why?" John wanted to know.

"Just work with me. Try it."

"Okay…. He was going to rehearsal," John offered.

"Good answer. Ken?"

"What?"

"Why did he have the Sousaphone?"

"I guess John's right: rehearsal."

"No… that's not the deal. You have to give a different answer."

"Oh…. I guess his kid's at rehearsal and he'd forgot the suzy-thing. Dad's bringing it to him." Ken stuck with the rehearsal theme.

"Another good answer…Larry?"

"Uh…. I guess he found it on the sidewalk and thought someone inside might own it."

"Okay… that's different. Here's mine: He doesn't know why either. He has a compulsion; every time he finds a Sousaphone in a pawnshop he buys it and takes it to the community center. He doesn't know why, he just does."

"That's pretty complicated," Ken complained.

"But it works. It fits the facts."

"Almost anything could fit the facts," John complained good-naturedly.

"So give me another reason."

"We gonna do this again?" Ken laughed. "Okay... when he was a kid he stole a Sousaphone from the community center and he's always felt guilty about it. Now that he's an adult he's trying to make amends by bringing back a new one."

"No, he's going to auditions for "The Music Man" and he didn't have a trombone," John offered.

"There's a theater in the community center?" Ken asked.

"Sure, why not?" John replied. "It fits the facts."

"Larry? Your turn."

"I don't know. We've covered just about everything," Larry floundered.

"Well maybe he was taking it as a donation for a silent auction? Or he had a blind date and he's using the Sousaphone as an identifier, you know, 'I'll be the guy with the Sousaphone...'"

"The white Sousaphone," Ken added, "Just in case there a couple of other guys there with Sousaphones."

"Maybe he was taking it to get fixed?" Larry asked, and everyone agreed that could be the case.

"Okay," John asked, "So why are we talking about some imaginary guy with a band instrument?"

"We're not. We're talking about the stories we make up that explain things. Most of the time, we make up stories that deal with fear. You might just have easily said the guy with the Sousaphone was coming to kill you," to John: "It would have fit the facts.

"When you wife does something you don't understand, I'll bet you nine times out of ten that rather than ask her why, you, rather, we all, just make up a story that explains it, that fits all the facts: like she did that because she doesn't respect me, because she doesn't love me. Whatever your fear is, that's why she did it.

"But here's the thing, for every story you tell yourself, that you convince yourself is true, there are a dozen other explanations that also fit the facts that have nothing to do with how she does or doesn't feel about you."

"So what you're saying is that when my wife yells and screams at me and I think it's because she's angry I'm supposed to think that maybe she's not angry, that there's another reason," John snorted.

"No, you could be right the first time. But she might also be scared of something, it could be that she's not particularly angry, but she finds yelling is the only way to get your attention. It could be that in her youth yelling was an acceptable way of communicating general frustration...

"I don't know, I'm just suggesting that the next time you think you know why she did or said something, think about the guy with the white Sousaphone."

CHAPTER 18

A BETTER MAN RE-IMAGINES HIS WIFE

A lot of people think that's a typo above, that the title should be "re-images." Re-imaging is the process of letting go of your assumptions about your wife, the stories you tell yourself about what she believes, what she wants, what she thinks about you, what she hates about you.

You stick your foot in a fire and it burns, funny how it works but you come to believe that all fires will burn you and you govern yourself accordingly. It's a great survival skill, kept your ancestors safe, but it doesn't do much good with your wife, or in any relationship.

Consider you asked Mary to join you for breakfast and she said "No," you're not stupid, you know we all do everything for a reason, and so your mind immediately fills in the blank that isn't there and comes up with, No, *I hate you.* No, *you are a spendthrift.* No, *I hate your table manners,* No, *I'd rather spend the morning with my lesbian lover.*

Whatever your fear is, you are going to put it in to the blank, regardless of what her real intentions are. At some time in the past she either said something or you interpreted her behavior to give you a reason, however slight, to believe you knew the dark, true, mean reason for her refusal to go to breakfast.

You may be right. I'll bet you're not. I never was, but you may be. I hope that works out for you. The odds are you are wrong, because your beliefs are assumptions. They are guesses based upon past experiences and fears.

You: **Hey Mary, let's go to breakfast.**

Mary: **No.**

You: **What is it with you and breakfast? Is it because _____?**

Mary: **What? You think _____. That is so typical. That's your biggest problem...** And so it goes.

It's called psychological projection. It's "the beauty or the hag" and "the lovers or the chalice." When you look at these images, they can be seen two ways, each depending on whether your focus is on the negative or the positive space.

I'll help you out a little, in the beauty/hag image the beauty is facing to your left, but looking over her right shoulder, she is wearing a hat with a feather in the front, a black fur stole on her shoulders exposing her upper chest, and a black choker around her neck. The Hag is in profile, facing left but cheated a little towards the observer. The choker is her mouth, the cheek line of the beauty is her nose, the ear of the beauty is her right eye. She has black hair, with a white hood and is wearing a black fur high up around her neck. The image, entitled "My wife and my mother-in-law" was created by Wm. Hill in 1916. In the second image, the white image is the chalice; the black image is the silhouette of two people facing each other.

In the same way, everything we say, (you, me, Mary) can be interpreted from either a negative or a positive context. "You look pretty today" can be construed to mean "you look like a pig most of the time." The odds of it being misconstrued are directly proportional to the odds that her fear is that she looks like a pig and/or that she thinks you think she looks like a pig.

So the goal is to try to hear everything your wife says in a positive way, and conversely, if you think something you have said can be misconstrued, to make your true meaning clear.

It could be Mary said no to breakfast because she wanted to make waffles.

With mirroring, when Mary said No, you would most profitably say something like,

YOU: **"Okay, no breakfast. Can you tell me more about "why"? I don't intend to debate you. I am not going to argue the point or challenge you. I want to understand you."**

And maybe she'll talk, maybe she won't. But if she does... remember: No Debate.

I used the word re-imagining above because sometimes we get so used to our negative interpretations, it get so wrapped up in how we know things are, and we are so far off base, that our view of our spouses is pure fiction, pure imagination, and to get out of that rut takes some new imagination.

You have to imagine that she loves you. You have to imagine that she wants to be with you. You have to imagine that she respects you. You have to imagine that she lives for your smile.

"Right," you say, sarcasm dripping like acid to the floor from a cracked battery casing.

But if you think about it, this is exactly what you did when you first met your spouse. In those heady days of romance, you didn't need proof she loved your smile you simply took it for granted.

When you first met, instead of assuming the worst when she said no to breakfast, you would have made some light rejoinder, and she would have responded in kind because you both trusted each other.[51]

Now, you say, *"Brother, have you been paying any attention at all? I KNOW she doesn't love me. I have ample reason NOT TO TRUTST her."*

And I say this is WHAT YOU BELIEVE, not WHAT YOU KNOW. You may be absolutely right. She may hate your guts, her every motivation might be born of vile intemperance, in which case you'll soon be well shut of her. I'm surprised you even bought the book.

But if her motivations are not as you imagine, and you continue to act as if they are, you will also soon be shut of her, and it may be a tragedy of miscommunication, misinterpretation and psychological projection.

And while you're at it, don't sweat the small stuff. So often in relationships it's the little things that drive us most crazy, the underwear on the floor, the toothpaste cap. I have an electric toothbrush with a head for her and a head for me and she was

---

[51] The Rowboat

always leaving her head on the machine after she brushed her teeth, whereas I, noble sort that I am, always took my head off.

At first I didn't notice, then I wondered why, then it began to bug me and as things grew more strained between us I realized that she left it on there because she didn't care. I wasn't important to her. It didn't just bug me anymore, it was a daily reminder of the incredibly low esteem by which I was held, and I reacted to that pain with anger, and soon, every morning and every night I'd look at that damn toothbrush and seethe.[52]

It took years for me to realize that she was not an evil genius that had spent countless hours divining the most Mephisthophelean of plots to jab at me, to kill me by a thousand cuts. Not only was she not an evil genius, she wasn't trying to jab me. She just didn't think about it.

Now, with the tools contained in this book, I could bring it up to her in a non-confrontational way, but then I couldn't, so of course things got worse.

So here's the tool: don't sweat the small stuff. Keep your underwear in the dirty clothes hamper, and don't take it as a personal attack every time you pick hers up off the floor. And I'm not busting your balls because it's all your fault. It's not. She's doing it too. She's got stories in her head about you, your motivations and your beliefs that are so off the wall and wrong they make Pee Wee Herman look like Mr. T.

---

[52] I removed the cap to be considerate, that's my reality. If I don't recognize her reality, then she has to be operating in mine. Therefore she knows it is considerate to remove the cap, and the story I tell myself is that if she's not removing the cap it's because she's being deliberately inconsiderate.

But you're the one who bought the book, you're the one who wants to be a better man and to save your marriage and one of the ways you do it is by letting go of the angst of what she does or doesn't do and focusing on what you can do.

Lead. She will follow.

THE CANDLE

This is what we can observe about a candle. The wick, once white, chars black and curls over. Wax drips down the side.

This is what some conclude: the wick burns. The wax? The wax melts, but it's still there. It's what keeps the wick up.

The reality is that it is the wax that burns. The wick is just the device that brings the melted wax up to the flame via capillary action.

The modern perception that it is the wick that burns is born of the self-tapering wick. You may have heard the phrase "tapering" before. It means the process of cutting off excess wick. Long ago wicks were made of ordinary twined cotton string. As the candle burned down, the wick would lay over into the pool of melted wax and eventually drown the flame. By tapering the wick before it was lit, simply snipping off all but a quarter inch, the candle would burn better.

Sometime in the mid-nineteenth century someone, whose identity I cannot discover, invented (possibly accidentally) the self-tapering wick. The wick, previously just a twined string of cotton, was instead made of braided material, and as all strands were not made equally, as the wick grew hot, one strand of the braid would shrink more[53] than the others, causing the wick to bend. As the wick bent out of the core of the flame, it became exposed to oxygen at the outside of the flame, and burned. Not just the wax, but the wick actually burned, leaving no extra wick to trim as the candle burned.

Most people "know" it's the wick that burns, it makes sense and it conforms to their observations. They believe it so they don't challenge it, but their belief is founded upon their misconstrued observations.

People often confuse what they believe and what they know. We believe something is right or wrong, but empirically, we cannot know that it is right or wrong.

Arguments about abortion stem from beliefs clashing. A believes that it is right for a woman to be able to chose. B believes that it is right for the fetus to live. Neither has a shred of evidence, any proof or any test to establish a factual foundation for their beliefs.

Both have spent a great deal of time thinking about the subject and have formed conclusions which are what they believe. When A tells B his conclusions are wrong, B takes offense, because A is essentially saying that B is an idiot, that he thinks wrong, that his values are skewed.[54]

---

[53] Or expand less, in this instance whether it is the hag or the beauty is irrelevant.

[54] Want to have some fun? The next time someone says something that goes against your beliefs, be it political, religious, or even outright bigotry, instead of keeping silent or arguing, say "So you believe….." and then "Tell me more." Mirror them and see where it leads.

Beliefs are hard things to change. Sometimes they are based upon what we have been taught all of our lives, sometimes they are conclusions we have reached by challenging and reconsidering, at great cost, those tenets that have been given to us. Sometimes they are based on our assumptions and our fears.

The same goes, in large measure, for what you "know" about your wife. If you allow yourself to challenge the beliefs you have formed about your wife, you will most assuredly find most, if not all, are projections.

CHAPTER 19

A BETTER MAN APPRECIATES OTHER'S REALITY

We all think we know what we are talking about. We all think we are right. The mythology of Superman (the comic, not some Freudian thing) has always included several individuals spotting something in the sky and shouting out,
"Look in the sky!"
"It's a bird!"
"It's a plane!"
"No, it's Superman!"
Cue the music.

The point is that each of the individuals looking up into the sky told the truth about what they saw. The one who thought it was a bird actually thought it was a bird. That's the way our mind works. We spot an anomaly, and we try to make it fit into patterns that we recognize. He probably thought he could see the wings flapping. Same for the guy who saw the plane.

We do the same thing in our relationships, we define events using our experience and we create a real image in our minds as about what has happened. This is our reality.

In the Superman example, the individuals make quick observations and they are not wed to them, they are not committed to them because there is no cost of any sort associated with being wrong. When the guy correctly identifies Superman, the others abandon their perceptions, see the issue more clearly, and agree.

Life doesn't work that way. In reality it would have gone more like,

> "Look, in the sky!"
> "It's a bird!"
> "It's a plane!"
> "It's a bird, you idiot, everyone can tell it's a bird."
> "It's Superman!"
> "Who asked you, Bub? Butt out. It's a plane, I tell ya. I've seen planes, I can recognize one when I see it."
> "Are you calling me a liar?"
> "No, I'm calling you a moron."
> "No, it was Superman."
> Cue the fight.

Our brain tries to connect the dots to form a pattern. It's why we can see shape of trees or houses in clouds, it how we can see the face of Jesus in a burnt piece of toast, it how we can make incredible leaps in our understanding of the universe, whether it's Newton and gravity or Einstein and the theory of relativity.

In relationships we do the same thing, and just like examples above, most of the things we see when we connect the dots are pure imagination. Occasionally we stumble across a truth, but most of the time we see the world from an intensely personal and unchallenged point of view.

Earlier I wrote about re-imagining your wife[55], about how you had created stories that explained to you why she did things, and how often those stories were wrong.

Honoring another's reality is similar, but exactly the opposite. In your own case, you have to challenge your pre-conceptions, but with others, you have to accept them.

---

[55] Chapter 18

You gotta be kidding me! First I'm supposed to forget everything I know about her and see her in the best possible light and now I'm supposed to accept all the hooey, all the unfounded crap she's got in her head about me?

In a word: Yes.

Exactly. I couldn't have said it better if I had written it myself. Well, almost.

You don't have to accept her reality, you don't have to buy into her ideas of who you are or what your motivations are, but you have to honor that she believes it to be true. She's not stupid. She's put the dots together in a way that makes perfect sense to her. If you challenge her reality you demean her, you tell her she is wrong.

Remember when you were a kid and there was a monster under the bed? Everything in your environment confirmed there was something under the bed. You heard it, you maybe even smelt it. And when your Dad came in and turned on the lights and made you look, did you, even for one moment, buy his line of hooey?

What did he know? Obviously the monster stepped out for a moment, or there was another rational explanation, because you KNEW the monster was there. It made perfect sense. Your dad proving you wrong did absolutely nothing to make you re-evaluate your position, and in fact simply reinforced your growing belief that he was either an idiot or in league with the monster.

So too, in relationships, you have too accept that their reality is born of the same rational process that you use to create your reality[56], and that challenging it is both counter productive and threatening. No one has ever, in the history of mankind, ever let go of a belief just because someone else told them they were wrong to believe it.

You accept their reality. You honor it. You mirror it. You give them the opportunity, and the safety, to re-examine it on their own time, and you give them, through your acceptance and your behavior as a better man, new dots to draw their picture from, and soon she will begin to see things differently.

I see Dan coming down the street I get a sick feeling in my stomach, because I have known Dan a while, and he has done a good many things over the years to convince me he that he dislikes me intensely. Ask me why I think he hates me and I'll tell you exactly how I know it. It will make sense to me, and if I tell it well it might make sense to you too.

It would do you no good to tell me I was wrong. It would do you no good to tell me, "Hunt, I know Dan and he doesn't dislike you. He doesn't even know you exist."

I know better. You are mistaken, and frankly, I don't trust you any more now that you're taking Dan's side of things.

You never get anywhere by challenging someone's reality. Consider the scenario where you come in from the yard and Mary gives you a look that you recognize as deadly. Immediately you are on the defense, because you know Mary is angry and dangerous.

YOU: **What?**

---

[56] Remember how the brain works, Chapter 6.

MARY: **You know.**

YOU: **No I don't know, Mary, how could I possibly know unless you tell me.**

MARY: **You were flirting with Carla.**

YOU: **What are you talking abut? I was just talking to her about her driveway. You have to be crazy to think I was flirting with her....**

And you begin the process of trying to disabuse her of what you call her silly notions but what she calls her reality, and it is not going to work, brother. To challenge her reality is to challenge her intelligence. None of us take that well. None of us appreciate it.

She saw you talking, she stirred it up with her fears about the troubles in your relationship and the fact that she finds you attractive so of course Carla does, plus she knows how Carla's mind works because of the stories they've shared and she wouldn't put it past the woman not to lead you to the bedroom.[57] She's put two and two together and she's very confident of her math.

Now, if you say[58]...

YOU: **I can tell you're upset. You are important to me and I want to understand you. Please tell me what's bothering you.**

---

[57] She's got a reptilian stem too, and it time she will come to recognize that, she'll learn to train her dog.
[58] Because you read Chapter 16 and you are not defensive, but rather embracing her anger.

MARY: **You know.**

YOU: **I don't, but I want to. Please tell me.**

MARY: **You were flirting with Carla.**

YOU: **What I heard you say was that you thought I was flirting with Carla. Tell me more.**

Now you have a conversation because you do not start off by telling her she is wrong. You aren't saying she's right, but you can see how it would make sense to her. You encourage her to talk about it, and before you know it she's telling you something important, something you never would have gotten had you just thrown up your hands, gone inside and opened a beer.

Okay, but how do I finish this thing? I can't leave her with the thought I was flirting with Carla. I'm not going to stop talking to my neighbors just because my wife has these crazy ideas.

In the process of mirroring the discovery process may go no deeper than a revelation of the physical behavior you innocently exhibited that alarmed her.

MARY: **"I didn't like the way you leaned into her, or the way you stood with your back to me."**

YOU: **"So, you didn't like the way I leaned towards her or that I had my back to you? Is that right?"**

MARY: **"Yes."**

YOU: **"Is there more?"**

MARY: **"You don't know...."**

Hey... you're getting this mirroring stuff down pretty good. Note that you didn't repeat exactly what she said, but you paraphrased it correctly. That works too.

You already know she's angry, so at some level you know she is hurt and/or afraid. So what did you learn with just this tiny bit of mirroring?

That leaning in towards someone is taken by your wife to be a sign of intimacy. It doesn't matter that Carla is, in Sinefeldian terms, a low talker[59]. That's an excuse, a justification of your behavior that, if you focus on it will allow you to remain "right," and when you're right you don't have to listen because they are the one who is wrong.

What matters is that your wife may have given you a great way to show her intimacy.... Lean in to her when you're talking. Maybe not. She could just be justifying her behavior, but it's worth a shot. You're not going to do yourself any harm to lean in towards her the next time you pay her a compliment or she shares something with you.

And you've learned that, maybe, next time it would be better to ask Carla to repeat what she said rather than leaning in to catch every word.

And you've learned that Mary cares for you: she's jealous.

And you've learned, not that you can't talk to your neighbors, but that when you do don't stand with your back to your wife and lean in to them, but not because you don't want to make

---

[59] Season 5, Episode 2, "The Puffy Shirt" 9/23/1993

your wife angry, not because you are caught by the short hairs and horribly pussy whipped, but because….. wait for it….

YOU DON'T WANT TO HURT HER and you now know, because of your mirroring, that her anger veiled the pain she felt when she thought you were flirting.

So you finish this by saying,

YOU: **"I can understand how my leaning into Carla and standing with my back to you gave you the impression that I was flirting with her, that makes sense to me, and I am going to keep your thoughts in mind the next time I talk to her, hell, the next time I talk to anyone."** (Here you lean in towards her.) **"Thank you for sharing this with me."**

MARY: **"Are you trying to start something, buster?"** (But she's smiling, and she's not talking about an argument, quite the opposite.)

Okay, that last bit is for the advanced group, and it's probably not going to happen to you first time up, but I promise you listening to your wife and accepting her reality and owning your actions have been proven, in my life, to be incredible aphrodisiacs. I shit you not.

CHAPTER 20

A BETTER MAN IS A LEADER

The old adage is lead, follow or get out of the way. In the context of your marriage that might be extrapolated to: Lead, stay in the miserable marriage as is, or get a divorce.

Since the premise of the book is to save the marriage, the second two options are not available. You must be the leader.

Leadership in a relationship is not about any ultra-orthodox religious belief that the man is the man and the woman is chattel. It is not about dictatorship, it is not about laying down the law. It's leadership, not pulling-ship, or dragging-ship, or forcing-ship. It is about showing the way, it is about learning new skills that you can share.

Above all, leadership is about knowing where you are going, because you cannot lead if you are wandering aimlessly about. In this instance you know where you are going: you goal is to save your marriage. That's why you bought the book. The path you are going to follow is to be a better man, and as you change you are blazing a trail that your wife and family can follow whether they have you in sight or not.

A leader in the relationship is the one who doesn't wait for the other to go first. A leader knows how to defuse confrontations. A leader in the relationship knows how to prevent conversations from devolving into confrontations. A leader in a relationship sets a good example for his children to follow. A leader in a relationship knows he isn't perfect and owns his mistakes. A leader in a relationship is aware of his anger and controls it. A leader in a relationship can set aside his preconceptions and see other's reality.

How can you become a leader? You can't. There are no classes. There are no applications to fill out, there are no permits or licenses, and there are no professional associations you can join. You don't become a leader, you are a leader. It is a state of mind which is the antithesis of "victim."

If you are a leader, you do the best you can at what you do, whether its man, husband, father or professional.

If you are a leader you seek understanding instead of recognition, you seek growth instead of stagnation, and you accept responsibility and let others seek recognition.

If you are a leader you do the things in this book, not for recognition, but because they are key to your growth and your improvement.

If you are a leader you do the things in this book regardless as to whether they get a response.

When you lead you blaze a clear trail, and you don't look back over your shoulder to see if others are following. If you leave a trail, they will follow.

A leader is someone others want to follow, that others want to emulate. You can be that man.

CHAPTER 21

A BETTER MAN DOESN'T HAVE A CRAZY WIFE

I have a friend who once wondered aloud if all women were crazy, or if he just drove every woman he dated insane. I'll give him credit for considering the possibility that he contributed to the problem, but note this well: a better man doesn't imagine his wife in pejorative terms. Crazy is an insult. Crazy is an abdication of responsibility. When a man says his wife is crazy, in one word he paints a picture whereby he is the innocent victim unable to meet the unfair and irrational demands of a mentally unbalanced spouse: if you posit that you can't do anything about it, you don't have to do anything about it. It's her fault.

Here's the truth of the matter: we all have our own peculiarities, our own phobias, our unreasoning fears, our assumptions of the inflexibility of the rules that govern our lives. For every fear there is a continuum, a linear progression from almost no fear at all to mildly incapacitating fear to totally incapacitating fear.

Consider this Tale of Two Howies....

Howie Mandel, a pretty good stand up comic, not a bad intern on *St. Elsewhere*, and a damn fine game show host on *Deal or No Deal*, is a self-admitted mysophobic, or as it is more commonly referred to, a germaphobe. He's possessed by a pathological fear of contact with dirt, germs, and contamination. He doesn't shake hands with people, he bumps fists. He shaves his head because it makes him feel cleaner, and he confesses he has a difficult time using any restroom other than his own.

Having said that: he is a husband of over 30 years; a father of three; and is successful in his profession. He is a highly-functioning mysophobic. He has found the ability to interact with society despite his fears; he has found the tools that allow him to succeed as a father, husband and professional.

I don't imagine that his condition is easy for his wife, his children or his employees, and yet, as near as I can tell, none of them say he's crazy. I imagine they appreciate the fact that he owns his mysophobia. He doesn't hide from it; he isn't in denial; he even jokes about it. I imagine his family appreciates that he seeks professional care and takes medication to help him control his mysophobia and I imagine they admire him for his successes in his struggle and have compassion for his failures.

Howard Hughes, on the other hand became so fearful of inhaling contaminants that he installed a massive aircraft-grade filtration system in the trunk his '54 Chrysler: that's a bit over the top. Somehow, possibly because of the times, possibly because of ignorance he never challenged his fear, he never owned his dysfunction, and he became a recluse. He used his money and influence to insulate himself from his fears, but in the process he ended up living alone in a hotel room, communicating with his subordinates by messages written on legal pads. He became so obsessed he would insist that a person with a stain on their shirt to remove the clothing or leave and he used tissues to pick up everything.

When he divorced in 1971 from his second (possibly third) wife, Jean, he had not seen her in over two years and they communicated only by phone. He cut his hair and nails only once a year and when he died in 1976 his emaciated body had to be formally identified by fingerprints because he is appearance was so far removed from the handsome, confident young man who had set transcontinental speed records, circumnavigated the globe, and was awarded a Congressional Gold Medal.

He was a good businessman, and he died one of the richest men in the world, but he lost his wife and arguably his sanity because he pandered to his fears, because he made his obsessions the most important things in his world.

In my continuum, Howard Hughes is probably as crazy as they come because my definition of crazy is when anyone lets their obsessions or fears destroy their happiness.

It's possible that your wife has a disability, an obsession or condition that not only allows you to think she's crazy, but probably drives you crazy too.

The first thing you need to do is to isolate your reaction to her behavior from her behavior. They are two different issues. You cannot control her behavior; you can only control your reaction to her behavior. Too often in relationships stressed by behavior problems that reaction is one of anger, hurt and frustration, compounded by the irreducible conclusion that this isn't fair. Well, too bad. It's what you got and you have to deal with it. If you don't want to deal with it, get a divorce, but understand even with a divorce as long as the kids are around you are going to be dealing with this one way or another, so you are not going to do yourself a disservice by starting now, while you're married, while you will have the best effect. Here's how to do it:

First off, it is okay to insist that your partner come to terms with and address the behavior issue. It is appropriate to require your spouse be Howie rather than Howard. If she isn't going to own her problem, if she isn't going to make her relationship with you more important than her relationship with her dysfunction, then she isn't going to bring her full packaged to the table, and under those circumstances, just like with addiction, you haven't got a marriage to save.

Having said that, walking in the door and saying "Honey, you have to change or I'm leavin'" isn't likely to work. At all. Before you can require your wife to undertake the scary work of changing, you have to clean up your side of the street first.

That means you have to stop reacting to her behavior. Becoming angry, dismissive, or patronizing not only doesn't modify her behavior, but it makes the situation worse. It isn't working for you: let it go[60]. You have to explore and understand her reality, you have to let go of judging her as "crazy."

Let's say Mary is, since we're on the subject, a germaphobe and you stop at a gas station where she, out of abject necessity, uses the restroom. It takes a while and when she returns she is visibly distressed.

In the first scenario you both get in the car, you sigh audibly and grumble about the time and your desire to get through Atlanta before the running of the bulls at rush hour. She picks up on your poorly concealed displeasure, takes it as a judgment, and responds with defensive anger. You shut up because you know you can't win the argument, but you drive on feeling misused and unappreciated... and so does she. Life really doesn't get sweater that this.

---

[60] Many will argue that doing the same thing but expecting different results is a sign of insanity. Fighting with her over her behavior does not, never has and never will effect a change in her. Again, let it go or sit down and consider which one of you is the crazy one.

In the second scenario when she gets in the car you say "I can tell you are upset. I know how difficult it is for you to use a public washroom. Do you want to tell me about it?" You invite dialog, you invite the discussion, you empathize with your wife even if it means sitting in traffic for an hour because, and this is important, an hour in traffic is less destructive to your marriage than hours, if not days, of sublimed anger and resentment.

Perhaps Mary says yes, and you mirror. Perhaps Mary says no and you say "I want to support you around this. Before we leave can I get you anything from the convenience store?" That last little bit is called consideration, also known as being nice. It's an amazingly effective tool for rehabilitating relationships.

In the first scenario you got caught up in your side of the story, about how you shouldn't have to put up with this crap, about how most of it was affected, about how she wasn't like this when you married, etc. As a result, you became judgmental, unsympathetic, and really, not a nice guy to be around. I wouldn't have wanted to be in the back seat.

In the second scenario you maybe took a lesson from American theologian Reinhold Niebuhr who was credited in a 1937 edition "The Intercollegian and Far Horizons" as the author of the Serenity Prayer. It's a big part of AA and other step programs to recover from addiction[61]. The concept of the prayer has been around for a long time[62] and is best encapsulated in the phrase "God, grant me the ability to accept the things I cannot change,

---

[61] Addiction? I think there are two kinds of addiction: chemical/biological dependency and habituation. In a way, your habit of responding to your wife is similar to an addiction: it interferes with your happiness, you don't think it's hurting anyone, you can't/don't control it, you lie about it and justify it to others... just a thought.

[62] There's a Mother Goose rhyme from the 17th century that conveys the same sentiment.

courage to change the things I can; and the wisdom to know the difference."

And you realized you couldn't change Mary, and simply accepted her as she was. With that acceptance, the refusal to rush to judgment, you give Mary safety and security, you give her one less thing to be angry about, you give her one less stressor, and in the process you make her life just a little bit easier, and with that breathing room Mary might be able to decide she wants to be more Howie than Howard.

Or, after you've let go of the judgment and the anger over her behavior, after she feels safer in your company, then perhaps you have the conversation where you tell her

YOU: **I love you, but I struggle with your germaphobia. I know it makes you unhappy, and it makes me so unhappy that I cannot continue in this relationship unless we learn how to better handle it. For the sake of our marriage and our children, I want you to ask you to seek a psychiatrist and if you do I will help you in any way I can.**

After you've done all the ground work of cleaning up your side of the street you have a much better chance that she is going to actually hear your concern and react accordingly. There's a chance she won't, but a negative response is infinitesimal smaller than if you used the original, "Honey, you have to change or I'm leavin'"

The better man is compassionate of his wife's dysfunctions. He asks how he can help. He is supportive; he is not judgmental or demeaning. Only in that way can he help her stay on the good side of the Howie-Howard line. A better man doesn't have a crazy wife because a better man helps her stay sane.

CHAPTER 22

SEX, DRUGS AND ROMANCE

SEX: Invariably, in every marriage on the rocks, and even some marriages that are doing fine, sex has become a distant memory, the thing others do, what you wouldn't mind doing to that woman you saw driving the Beemer, but it is not something that you do with any amount of frequency or satisfaction with you wife.

Here's what I know about that: Nada. Zippola. Sex crept out of my marriage and out of a failed relationship and closed the door so softly that I can't say when the end began. I can say only that one day it dawned on me that we hadn't had sex in a while, and it didn't look like we were going to have sex in the near future and that was alright by me.

It wasn't that I didn't want it, it was that I didn't want to go there. I didn't want to re-embrace the intimacy, I didn't want to be rejected, I didn't want all the work for an orgasm I could give myself.

The story I was telling myself was that I was bored with our sex life, been there and done that. Worse, I didn't feel appreciated, or wanted. I often felt as if sex was, for her, a chore, and that was a major turn off. I never asked her if sex was a chore. I observed her reactions and made conclusions which I relied upon. I told myself a story and to my detriment I believed it.

I now know this: for me, sex is important, great sex is born of intimacy. Intimacy comes from sharing thoughts, emotions, fears and hopes. When you stop sharing, when you begin to isolate, to withdraw from your partner, sex becomes a ritual, devoid even of the gratification of the conquest. So even though I was accepting of the absence in my life, it was a self-destructive concession.

How do you get your sex life back on line? I do not know. I suspect that in many relationships the process is organic. It slowly comes, part and parcel with the restoration of trust and affection[63]. In other's it will take more work, and if so it may involve a sex therapist[64], but if you are both committed, your sex life can be rekindled.

There is one thing I do know about sex: if sex is important to you then you can't sit around like I did, make assumptions, and never address the issue. You have to talk about it. Scary, yes, but essential. If it then turns out it is simply not in the cards, not only has she told you it isn't going to happen but you also believe her, then you have to decide whether you are going to leave or stay. Don't fool yourself that you can get your needs met outside the marriage, even if she agrees. There is no middle ground. You either have to walk away from the sex life or the marriage.

DRUGS: Not social drugs (a misnomer: I have never known drugs to promote social behavior.) But good, old-fashioned anti-depressants. A lot of guys don't believe in drugs.

---

[63] Appendix C

[64] Get your mind out of the gutter. Nothing like that happens. It's therapy designed to re-kindle your affection and intimacy, it's about learning to trust. It's about learning how to communicate about something we've been taught not to talk about.

Perhaps the disdain stems from a perceived stigma attached to mental health issues, perhaps the dislike finds its roots in a "natural body" concept whereby one believes the body has the ability to heal itself and that unnatural substances pollute our delicate micro-ecosystem and destroy our ability to balance ourselves. Perhaps the revulsion comes from a more tough it out, pull yourself up by your bootstraps sort of macho mentality.

All that makes as much sense to me as starving yet disdaining the use of a shot gun to bring game to the table because you want to do it the natural way and kill the wild boar bare handed; or passing on a box-end wrench because you want to get the bolt out the old-fashioned way: with your fingers; or taking a rain check on the cast and crutches because the compound fracture in your tibia will probably heal just fine; or opting for the cave over the condo.

Here's my thought on the matter: if you are depressed and you are not using every tool available to you to beat it, then not only are you doing yourself a great disservice, but you are damaging your family, who have to live with your sad, self-indulgent, Neolithic self.

Having said that, you might not be a sad, self-indulgent troglodyte. A good many people don't know they are depressed. They think that feeling helpless, hopeless, worthless, and pessimistic, along with trouble sleeping, fatigue and perhaps the occasional suicidal ideation is absolutely normal. I know I did.

It took a crisis at work, where I thought I stood to lose everything I had, to make me seek help, and like most people I went to my family doctor. I love my doctor. I think he gives me great care, but I have to tell you that going to a general practitioner for help with depression is the functional equivalent of dropping off your Lamborghini at Goober Pyle's service station[65].

Initially, it might be your only option. If you're stuck in Mayberry you need to get back on the road so you can get your car back to the dealership, back to the guys who studied in Italy.

My family doctor gave me a prescription for what ever the last pharmaceutical salesman had been pushing, and it worked. It had horrible side effects, but it worked. I started seeing options that had been obscured by malaise, I started feeling hopeful, and I stopped snapping at every frustration.

One morning I walked onto my front porch and heard birds singing, and it stopped me cold because, since I couldn't remember when, I couldn't recall noticing birds singing. I had been in a tunnel of gloom for so long I had stopped taking pleasure from life.

But the side effects, whew…. There were some sexual side effects that were definitely interfering with my ability to takes some very specific pleasures from life, and to resolve that I went to a prescribing psychologist, to a man who did nothing but study the vast pharmacology, both through the literature and through his own research, in an effort to discover the most effective medication, or combination of medications, for his patients.

It took months, and several weird combinations of drugs, but we finally came up with a regimen that allowed me to get my life back on track.

---

[65] The Andy Griffith Show, CBS, 1960 - 1968

Some might react to this story with horror. Just the thought of taking anti-depressants is bad, but entertaining the idea that you might have to take them for the rest of your life is as scary as an alcoholic trying to envision a life with never another drink.

I view the drugs as a crutch, as something to help you keep your balance as your body heals. With a bad break, you might be using the crutches for years, with a horrid injury you might always need a cane, but in most cases, you'll lose the crutch, you'll lose the limp, and your life will get back to where you want it to be.

Most professionals say that depression is defined as having five or more symptoms for two weeks. The emotional symptoms include feeling sad, futile, hopeless, worthless, and pessimistic, the physical symptoms include agitation, irritability, trouble sleeping, excessive sleeping, weight gain or loss, fatigue, and behaviors like avoiding social interaction, hobbies, sex, as well as anger or discouragement.

That was my life. I thought it was just the way things were. Look back over the past few months and inventory what's been going on in your life. If you have been consistently irritable and angry, depression could be the cause. If you have been tossing and turning at night for weeks on end, or feeling hopeless and discouraged on a daily basis, you are not going to do yourself a disservice by considering your alternatives.

A life-long friend came to me and stated he was an alcoholic and that he was never going to drink again. I didn't think he had a problem. He drank, sure, and he got drunk now and then, but he'd never been ticketed for DUI, I'd never seen him drinking at inappropriate times, and as far as I could tell drinking wasn't interfering with his life, which included a wife and five wonderful kids.

But what could it hurt? Not taking a drink again had very little downside for him. Maybe for me, because I'd enjoyed sharing a beer and a game of pool with him, and that was going to change.

He identified a problem in his life and took steps to correct it. I admire him for it. I encourage you to do the same thing. If there is even the possibility some of your unhappiness stems from depression act on it. See your doctor and see if it works for you, see if it helps.

Clearly, nothing else you have done so far has helped. So why not try.

And as it turned out, I was wrong about my friend. He had been hiding his drinking for decades; he started in the morning and maintained a buzz all day long, every day of the week. I never saw it, perhaps, because I had never truly seen him sober. In the same way, I never thought I had a problem with depression, because I had been unhappy for so long that it just seemed the way things were supposed to be.

ROMANCE: Romantic love, that time when you couldn't see enough of her, that time when just a glimpse of her made your hear beat faster, where you experienced an inchoate sense of joy just by being near her, where erections were easy to come by (no pun intended) and lasted forever, where holding hands was almost as good as being naked under the sheets.

You may never see that again.

The good news is that you are also probably done with acne, you voice has changed, and you are never going to look off a hotel balcony and think "How cool would it be to jump from here to the pool?"

Romantic love is essentially chemical, it's nature's way of getting men and women together for procreation, and afterwards it fades so the guys can finally get out of the cave and back to hunting wooly mammoths.[66]

True: it fades in six months to two years, which was very helpful when the species was protected by mixing up the gene pool as much as possible, but in today's world it just doesn't suit. Cavemen didn't need to become better men: they died before they were twenty-five. Their whole purpose was to populate the world, and they couldn't fulfill that mandate if they were getting involved with long term commitments.

Evolution changed the way we have to be. We live longer now, we have the opportunity to be more than simple hunters, we can look at the stars and see more than pinpoints in the membrane between earth and hell and actually comprehend not only our solar system, but galaxies, the universe, and esoteric things like dark matter.

Likewise, today we have time to look into ourselves and see not just a hunter, but something more, something with a soul, something with a value that transcends our limited concepts of biological life, something that needs to be nurtured to grow. (That's you, brother.)

Thus, where as our caveman forefathers were primarily attracted by fertility, (and let's not kid ourselves a nubile blond will still turn our heads) we, as theoretically more evolved creatures, are drawn to those individuals that compliment our weaknesses, that provide us with the opportunity for the conflicts that will allow

---

[66] This relates back to your greatest of all grandfathers and the way pleasure works. Chapter 2.

ourselves to grow. And come about six to twenty-four months, the chemicals wear off and we begin to chafe against the many characteristics that attracted us.

And that's the way it's supposed to be.

So, the odds are you are never going to get the loopy feeling of love you had before, the crazy hormone driven yen to mate that you feel with the good-looking saleswoman from Topeka (at least, that's where mine came from.) You are not going to have a crush on your wife again.

And that's not a bad thing.

Mature love is about common differences, it's about new frontiers, it's about support, it's about challenge, it's about growth, it's about acceptance. In mature love, you embrace the many things that separate you because they allow you to experience new things. In mature love, by letting go of your fears, you can go places you've never been before. For some, that's Highlands North Carolina. For others it might be a pedicure, for fewer still, a vegan cruise to Singapore. At some time, it is going to be a painful discussion, at another, it will be the liberating knowledge the bad thing that happened way back when doesn't have to rule your life, and in yet another it might mean simply accepting that your wife is always going to freak when a glass breaks, and knowing that that's okay. Whatever the experience is, it is a learning one.

In mature love you have a partner who accepts you for who you are, and who appreciates the person you strive to be. In mature love you are challenged daily to take the steps that transform you from caveman to modernman. (Write that down.)

So, if you are looking for this book to put the ZING back into your relationship, to make you're eyes pop and your heart race, that won't happen…. But if you learn to accept your wife as she is and to appreciate the things she wants to become, if you embrace your differences and let go of the fears then, brother, get ready for a ride your teenage, caveman mind never comprehended. It is a rush.

SAND CASTLES

The kid spent the best part of the morning building the castle on the rug in the den. He used the long blocks for the base, made arched colonnades with the cylinders, used the square and rectangular pieces to fill in the walls, and when all was done, every block was used and the castle stood almost as tall as he.

In the summer the young boys built a sand castle just above the high water mark. They used real shovels and buckets, formed the walls with a wooden grid and packed the sand in tightly. They formed a wall around the perimeter, then dug a semicircular moat before that, and as the tide began its inexorable return they carved the walls with painstaking care creating windows, stairways, and parapets. Dried sea oats became flagstaffs and driftwood was fashioned into drawbridges and portcullises. One scraped the courtyard smooth with a sea angle shell, and just as the first spent wave dribbled weakly into the moat the boys stood back and admired their work.

The woman placed the penultimate tile into the 10,000 piece puzzle, and then savored the last before placing it in the seemingly gaping hole to complete the picture and culminate hours of patient work. She stood to get a better angle and gazed with great satisfaction at the cardboard mosaic before her...

Then she pulled it apart and put it back into the box.
The kid knocked down the fort.
The tide washed away the sandcastle.

Some things are meant to be temporary. Life, the physical life we experience, is temporary.

Relationships are temporary. Compared to relationships, sandcastles are the great pyramid of Cheops. The fort is the Rock of Gibraltar; the puzzle is the Mona Lisa.

Tides come in, just to go out. You make up the bed, but only for the day, no more, it's just a temporary condition.

It is in the process of creating the puzzle, or the fort, or the sandcastle that we learn, and if we leave the fort standing, we can never create another, if we varnish the puzzle we can never reassemble it, and if we try to prevent the tide from erasing the castle we are doomed to failure.

Your relationship to your wife is temporary. It is going to end. You cannot maintain the status quo; you cannot keep the tide from rising.

But even as your relationship with your wife is ending, you are building a new one. Using the same logs, you can put together a different fort. Using the knowledge gained from the first, the second will be better. Each of you is changing. With each change the relationship that was is no more.

If sandcastles stood forever, the beach would be a horrible place to go. There'd be no where to lie down, no place to sit, and if relationships didn't change and grow we would soon find ourselves moribund and miserable.

But you've been there, so you know that.

CONCLUSION

The conclusion is that this is just the beginning. If you are intentional about being a better man, if you can commit yourself to controlling your reactivity and your anger, if you can become an active listener and a master of mirroring, while making decisions from a positive energy, and keeping your side of the street clean, all this while leading and being happy… if you can do all that, hell, I'd like to buy you and your wife a drink some day.

Cy Timmons is a wonderful singer that lives in the Mountains of North Carolina. Years ago he played at "The Tree on Peachtree" in Atlanta, and later in his own place, The Café Erehwon. Cy doesn't remember me. How could he? The water in the river always remembers the banks that chart its course, but the banks see the water all the time.

In the course of his sets Cy always had to deal with drunks and hecklers, and I was always amazed by his repartee, his vast repertoire of comebacks that would silence the uncouth among his customers. Once I had the opportunity to ask him how he maintained his cool, how he always was ready for with a comeback.

Cy laughed and related that it took practice. Early on he'd get hazed and it would flummox him completely, take him off his stride and mess up his performance. He said, like all of us, it wasn't until the next day that he slapped himself on the forehead and said "damn, that's what I should have said."

The next time the same heckle came, he usually forgot what he should have said, the third time, he got off a retort, but delivered it poorly, then the fourth, and so on until eventually it became part of his act. He almost depended upon the hecklers to be his straight men, to set up his zinging replies.

And every now and then, he would still get caught off guard by a heckler and have to do it all over again.

In this journey to be a better man you are going to drop the ball. You are going to get flummoxed. You are going to find yourself, like Cy, much after the fact saying "That's what I should have said! That's what I should have done." The key isn't that you dropped the ball, but that you pick it up and are resolved not to drop it again.

By the same token, you are going to be changing your life. Your wife is going to notice. At first you are going to see small changes, maybe some big changes, but then, sure as God made green apples, just when you think you got this thing licked, she is going to revert into that horrible thing you thought you recognized at the beginning of this journey and you are going to despair.

It's because she is scared. Change is frightening. You lived in misery for years simply because the hell you knew was marginally better than the hell you could imagine. You had abandoned any thought of joy in your life and were resigned to a tedious painful existence.

So, at some point, more than once, because change is unsettling, because the hell she knew was marginally better than any she could imagine, because she is afraid to embrace joy for fear of having it taken away again, she is going to revert back into old bad habits that were effective when you were fighting, when you weren't happy, when misery was your watch word.

If you are patient, if you are the best man you can be, it will pass. Stick to the plan. Stay the course. Think up a few more catch phrases that mean the same thing and insert them here.

I promise you that if you are honest with yourself, if you make being a better man your focus, if you pay attention to your mistakes and conscientiously do what you know you should do, you will save your marriage. If not this one, then definitely the next.

THE AWARENESS TEST

If you haven't seen this, you simply have too.

Go to my blog: bettermanbettermarriage.blogspot.com and hit the red link on the right that reads: Awareness test.

Or you can type either of the addresses below into your browser:

http://www.youtube.com/watch?v=Ahg6qcgoay4
http://www.youtube.com/watch?v=3RVJMSdIYaQ

Or you can just Google THE AWARENESS TEST, but the headlines are going to blow it for you.

Do it.

Take the test.

Then, and only then, turn the page.

I'm not going to walk you around the barn on this one, hoping you'll find the door. We'll walk straight in.

Too many times in our lives we become so focused on certain issues, whether it is something simplistic as to who took out the garbage, or who isn't doing enough to save the marriage, or who needs to change or whatever it is, we become completely unaware of the bear, and the bear you are ignoring in your relationship is your contribution, your own unwillingness to be the best man you can be.

Becoming aware of the bear in the Reality Test is a lot easier than becoming aware of the bear in your relationship, and that's because you have spent most of your marriage, indeed, most of your life, learning how to ignore the bear. You have trained yourself to ignore your contribution, and one of the tools that you use is hurt.

Your spouse says something that is undeniably mean, or she acts in a way that blindsides you with bad behavior, and you are hurt. After all I've done, she does this. Pang. You feel it.

And your first reaction is righteous indignation, "this is not fair" you think, and you don't get much past it. You lash out, you react, you strike back as you strive to claw your way to the moral high-ground[67] and even if you may not say it, you think and she hears[68] "you've got some nerve…"

And in the process of venting your hurt you completely overlook the bear in the room, which is your contribution.

---

[67] As if you've ever won an argument by proving you were right
[68] Remember, eighty percent of communication is non-verbal. She can interpret your sigh, you eye-roll, your slumped and dejected shoulders.

EPILOGUE

A BETTER MAN CAN NOT DO THIS ALONE

A crazy person thinks he is the only sane person in the world. By the same token, there are not many of us who can see ourselves, our actions, and our motivations objectively. When we reason out a mathematical problem it's fairly easy to come to a correct answer because we know the rules, we know the theorems, and we know how to double check ourselves as we go along.

Relationships, not so easy. There are no rules. I don't think anyone really tries to do the mean things, to cause the pain, and to join into the arguments that ruin a marriage. When we do things, it's generally because it makes sense to us. It seems fair. It seems justified.

So it is difficult to look back at your behavior and find fault with yourself.

Thus you need a friend, someone who can listen to you, someone who can sympathize with you, someone who can encourage you, someone who can catch you in your half truths and rationalizations.

This may be the hardest thing you've ever done, because as a rule, guys don't talk. We tend to share information: statistics from games; fact patterns from case scenarios; jokes. A guy says "my wife left me." And another guy says "Bummer. Did you see what the Pats did over the weekend?"

You are never going to hear that guy say, "Your wife left you? How does that make you feel? Tell me more."

Genetically, we are hunter gatherers. Our priorities are "can he kill a deer" not "how does he feel." We focus on performance, in bed, on the job, and on the playing field, but not in relationships.

There are two ways you can find the support you need to become a better man, to be the best man you can be.

The first is to buy a dozen copies of this book, pass them out to your friends, and invite them over to your house once a week. You sit in a rough circle so you can see each other, and then one by one you introduce yourself, you identify by name the woman in your life, and your kids, you state an appreciation you have for your wife, you state an issue you are struggling with, whether it's a frustration with her, and whether you'd like time to discuss it.

You limit this check in to about five minutes a man, and then after everyone's had his say you go back to the first person who needed time and you talk about it.

That's the process in a nutshell. It's so easy a blind monkey could do it, but in all honesty I'd put your success rate at about… Zero.

You need a moderator, you need a guide, someone who has been professionally trained to facilitate the discussion, to gently nudge the process along, to keep the participants polite and in line, as well as to direct the conversations away from non-productive foci. You need someone who not only knows how to mirror, but practices it and teaches it.

I have no stake in this, I get no dime, so believe me when I say, to get a moderator, go to the Imago web site and find a certified practitioner in your area and tell that man you want to start a Clearing Group. He will know what you're talking about, in fact, there may already be one up and running in your area.

Making that call is so easy a blind monkey could do it with one hand tied behind his back, and in all honesty I'd put your success rate at about... eighty-five percent. I'd give you more, but it is a tough thing to do. About fifty percent of the men who visit my group for the first time never come back for a second.

They don't come back because this is something they've never seen before, and they feel uncomfortable with it. They don't come back because they aren't committed to saving their marriage, but want to appear to have gone through the steps. They don't come back... For every guy that doesn't come back there's probably a different reason.

I'm betting that since you've read this far, you're not one of those guys, but I could be wrong, so that's why I knocked off the fifteen percent.

It ain't easy, but you can do it. You can be a better man. You can be happy. You can save your marriage.

I shit you not.

Oh... Remember that guy in Chapter 2 who left his wife because of anger... They were coming to my house for a party. It would be the first time she met me, as well as a couple of other men from the gathering. On the way over she said, "I'm not sure I want to go." And his first thoughts were *Great. What crap. You had to bring it up when we were almost there. Why did you even get in the car?* [69] And he knew why she pulled the stunt: she never wanted to come in the first place, she didn't like and resented his friends, and this was just her typical controlling behavior. At another time, he might have said just that and you can imagine the argument that would follow.

Instead of reacting, he paused, and then mirrored. "So what I hear you saying is that you're not sure you want to go. Is there more?"

And she said yes, and began to tell him how scared and nervous she was, how she feared what the guys knew about her and what they thought of her, all of which he mirrored. [70]

And he said: "That makes perfect sense to me. I'd be scared too." She smiled, grateful to have been heard and he offered his support and said "Why don't we give it a shot, and if you're not comfortable we will leave."

They came, and she had a great time.

---

[69] We all have unbidden thoughts, no matter how much we improve. They are the product of a lifetime of training and do not go away. The key is to pause, to let go of the reactivity, and to then enter the conversation conscientiously.

[70] And then summarized, and empathized… it's all in Chapter 17. I've abbreviated the conversation because I know you're ready to go.

APPRECIATIONS

At the end of each Clearing, we each choose someone in the room and appreciate what they have brought to the group, either through their participation, their growth, their insight, or even for just being who they are.

So it's appropriate before I close to appreciate those who have brought me to where I am. If you want to think of this as a dedication, you can. Hell, I put the Preface after the Introduction and started on Chapter 2. I can put the dedication at the end.

I mentioned Harville Hendrix, but I can't imagine he got to where he is alone, so I truly want to appreciate those people who are part of his life, who help him to be the best man he can be, especially his wife, Helen Hunt, who understands his affection for all things Trek.

I've mentioned Bob, Sulaiman and the Clearing, and they bear appreciation again. My first introduction to Imago was through Wendy Palmer Patterson,[71] and through her I was exposed to a "Getting the Love You Want" couples weekend, and I gotta say it was transformational. Go. It changed my life and I am thankful.

I want to appreciate Susan, my ex-wife, for sharing twenty-six years with me. When we divorced I struggled with what to do with my good memories, what to do with the joy we had shared. I didn't understand, I couldn't comprehend where it fit in my

---

[71] Yes, there's a connection there and it is the logical one

new life. I came to understand (and it may be the next book) that once we love, we always love. It may get buried in angst, anger or bitterness, but we hurt only because we love. Once I realized that, it all fit. So I want to apologize to Susan for every tear I brought, say thank you for all my countless smiles, and wish her well.

And I want to appreciate Angela, the woman in my life, who takes the time to enjoy. She is the only person, other than myself, who has read everything I've written and her love and support make me feel valued beyond all measure.

And I want to appreciate several others who have shaped my thinking, in no particular order:

> Willie R. Cox
> The men of The Clearing
> Lee Kahn
> Loren Solomon
> Patrick Callaway
> John Elliott
> Carrie Jones
> Isung Ju

BIBLIOGRAPHY OF A SORT

My bibliography is not going to be the academic symphony it might once have been. GOOGLE allows us to type in three words and find a million sites, at least a third of which are on point. So I'll just list the titles and the authors that have inspired me without regard to such common delimiters as alphabet or chronology, but where the books are on my shelf.

Getting the Love You Want, Harville Hendrix,
Perfect Love, Imperfect relationships, John Welwood
Parent Power, John Rosemond**
Keeping the Love You Find, Harville Hendrix
Rekindling Desire, Barry & Emily McCarthy
The Power of Now, Eckhart Tolle
The Joy Diet, Martha Beck
Getting to Yes, Fisher, Ury & Patton**
The Thing About Life is that One Day You'll be Dead,
            David Shields
What Happy People Know, Dan Baker and Cameron Stauth
The One Minute Manager,
            Kenneth Blanchard and Spencer Johnson**
Attacking Anxiety and Depression, Lucinda Bassett
Feel the Fear and Do It Anyway, Susan Jeffers
The Drama of the Gifted Child, Alice Miller
The Heart of the Soul, Gary Zukav and Linda Francis
His Needs, Her Needs, Willard Harley
Love Busters, Willard Harley
The Five Languages of Love, Gary Chapman
The Last Word on the Gentle Art of Self-Defense, Suzette Elgin
Skills for Success, Soundview Executive Book Summaries
How to Work a Room, Susan RoAnne

Home Dog, Richard A.Wolters**
Family Dog, Richard A.Wolters**
Radical Forgiveness, Colin Tipping
Men are from Mars, Women are from Venus, John Gray*
Relationship Rescue, Phil McGraw*
The One Minute Manager, Blanchard & Johnson**

And maybe half a dozen that I have lent out to friend and can't remember.

The only ones I read prior to my divorce are starred. The ones I read before my divorce but didn't truly appreciate are double starred.

APPENDIX A

Here are some "feeling" words to help you fill in the blank. More feeling words can be found in your dictionary.

abominable	calm	despicable	enthusiastic
absorbed	certain	determined	excited
accepting	challenged	detestable	fascinated
aching	cheerful	devoted	fatigued
affectionate	clever	diminished	fearful
afflicted	close	disappointed	festive
afraid	coerced	discouraged	forced
aggressive	cold	disgusted	fortunate
agonized	comfortable	disillusioned	free
alarmed	comforted	disinterested	frightened
alienated	concerned	dismayed	frustrated
alive	confident	dissatisfied	glad
alone	confused	distressed	gleeful
amazed	considerate	distrustful	good
angry	content	dominated	great
anguished	courageous	doubtful	grieved
animated	cowardly	down	guilty
annoyed	cross	dynamic	happy
anxious	crushed	eager	heartbroken
appalled	curious	earnest	helpless
ashamed	daring	ecstatic	hesitant
attracted	dejected	elated	hopeful
bad	delighted	embarrassed	humiliated
bitter	depressed	empty	hurt
blessed	deprived	encouraged	important
bold	desolate	energetic	impulsive
bored	despairing	engrossed	incapable
brave	desperate	enraged	incensed

indecisive	optimistic	sorrowful	worried
indifferent	overjoyed	spirited	wronged
indignant	pained	strong	
inflamed	panicked	stunned	
infuriated	passionate	sure	
injured	pathetic	surprised	
inquisitive	peaceful	suspicious	
insensitive	perplexed	sympathetic	
inspired	pessimistic	tearful	
insulted	playful	tenacious	
intent	pleased	tender	
interested	positive	tense	
intrigued	powerless	terrible	
irate	preoccupied	terrified	
irritated	provocative	thankful	
joyous	provoked	threatened	
jubilant	quiet	thrilled	
kind	reassured	timid	
liberated	rebellious	tormented	
lifeless	receptive	tortured	
lonely	rejected	touched	
lost	relaxed	unbelieving	
lousy	resentful	uncertain	
loved	reserved	uneasy	
loving	restless	unhappy	
lucky	sad	unsure	
merry	satisfied	upset	
miserable	scared	useless	
misgiving	secure	victimized	
mournful	sensitive	vulnerable	
nervous	serene	warm	
neutral	shaky	wary	
nonchalant	shy	weary	
offended	skeptical	wired	
open	sore	wonderful	

178

APPENDIX B

Over the years the men of The Clearing have come to formulate a few statements, aphorisms, and observations which try to encapsulate the essence of our emerging understand of who we are and how we become better men.

Several are the basis for this book; others are presented here for your consideration. Credit for the thoughts go to the men, credit for recording of the thoughts goes to David K

Where you are is the only place you can be right now! Δ Choose your mood (mind set) before you interact Δ **What you do is the only thing you can control** Δ Our reactions are valuable windows into ourselves that must be looked through to become better men Δ If you choose to stay in the relationship you must do the work in the relationship Δ **If someone else has done it, chances are it is possible** Δ Eliminate the "bitch" word from your vocabulary Δ If you find yourself in a situation that stresses you out, first, check your attitude, look outside the box. Try to find a deeper, more basic reason than the current event(s) Δ Geographic therapy (moving) doesn't work: no matter where you go, there you are Δ Failure to accept personal responsibility is fear based and controlling Δ Humility – associated with the acceptance of responsibility – is strength Δ Shaming – blaming for behavior – is weakness Δ Controlling behaviors are at their core violent: withdrawal; isolation; yelling and screaming; cursing; throwing things; criticizing; interrupting; ignoring; accusing; sarcasm; depersonalizing; name calling; blaming; lecturing. Δ **Move out of your head and into your heart** Δ Be very aware of how you see the people in your life. Make the conscious decision to eliminate negative terms and views Δ If there is any negativity about a person, see it as negative behavior then let it go Δ If you are not sharing, you are not intimate Δ Your partner may not, initially, respond in any way Δ Wallowing in our "history" enables us to avoid our current issues. Δ **Sometimes when you win you lose** Δ Vulnerability is truly strength. The tree that bends to the wind does not break Δ If our spouse acts in such a way that says she is fearful or needs safety, alleviate the fear and make them feel safe Δ **The disconnect between what you do and what you ought to do creates destructive conflict within** Δ The very traits we can't stand in our partners are the ones that we possess Δ Respecting another person includes not expecting them to take care of you Δ Recognizing and "speaking" the love language of your partner is an act of respect and love Δ **The worst thing that can happen by working to be a better man is that you will be a better man** – John Δ It is all about doing the little things that you can as well and as lovingly as possible...then let go Δ Be there for your partner to understand her reality Δ **It is never the wrong time to reach out** i.e. contacting friends and family, checking in, saying I love you Δ Misery, depression, angst and pain pervert our view of an otherwise wonderful world Δ The goal often interferes with the journey Δ **Unconditional love is co-dependent and enabling. Adult relationships are always conditional, always have boundaries** Δ Throw the ball correctly and once it leaves your hand, let go of it mentally and emotionally Δ **The advice you desperately wish to give is generally the advice you need to accept** Δ The things you want to ignore are the very simple and scary things you have to face Δ **When something is not working stop and try something else** Δ We are responsible for all of our choices Δ Demonstrating "solidarity" with our partners builds trust and safety for them Δ In any situation, you will be doing some kind of growth work Δ Analyzing her behavior is avoidance Δ If your partner has "too much power" it is because you are giving it away Δ **Sarcasm Is Violence** Δ You are only responsible for your own behavior △ **Control is an illusion** – let go and use the energy elsewhere △ You are only responsible for your truths △ Your partner's reactions cannot kill you and should not control you △ Show appreciation whenever possible and tell the giver how it makes you feel △ An absent (physically or emotionally) father has a bad impact on kids △ **Avoidance does not work** △ Allow your partner to be who she is and to own her own stuff. Her truths are hers △ **Criticism kills (relationships)** △ We cause our own pain △ **You cannot make your partner happy. You CAN make yourself happy** △ Own your growth △ **When you are complimented take time and allow yourself to be appreciated, don't demure or disparage yourself, embrace it and return thanks** △ Defensiveness and/or contempt are relationship killers. △ Understanding changes our "experience" of our partner △ **Pain is a 'wake up call** △ Part of our growth and transition is learning to live with the loss of the old behavior △ Never equivocate △ If our role in our relationship is rigid it stifles us and the relationship △ **There is ALWAYS a choice!** △ Our past often separates us from our present △ First, decide first where you are going … then go △ We will see what we are looking for. We notice what we want to notice. Learn to "want to see" things that promote your own personal growth. △ **You must be what you wish the world to be** △ Follow your discomfort to find out what you are hiding from yourself! △ **Avoiding the pain allows the pain to get stronger** △ Keep your commitments. Your word is your integrity △ Manhood is about 'Improving' –Bob P. △ **"One of these days" actually means "None of these days". Do it now** △ Decisions made from fear are disempowering △ There is no set time table for anyone's healing. It happens as it happens and it needs to be allowed, encouraged and supported △ The problems we have with our spouses are the problems we have with the world △ **In the particular lies the general** - John C △ We always have the choice of how we react △ **Appreciating your spouse is** only half the job – the other half is **TELLING them** Δ If you retreat from discomfort, you miss opportunities Δ Until your partner is sure that you understand the magnitude and importance of their feeling(s) they will keep up whatever "anger behavior" they are doing Δ You never really know the full and far reaching effect(s) you have on people Δ **Leave home, grow up, be who you want to be** Δ Care for yourself – rather than looking to others to care for us Δ **Trust is a gift. It can never be earned** Δ Healthy communication is non-manipulative. Δ If you do what you have always done, you will get what you have always gotten! Δ **What works at work doesn't work at home** – Hunt Δ Listen to the excuses you give to avoid change, for they are keys to understanding yourself and becoming a better man Δ **It takes two to play a game** Δ Fear Nothing - Carl W Δ Deal with stuff earlier rather than later. It may be easier to apologize than to ask acceptance – but it doesn't do good things for relationships Δ Being a good parent necessarily involves being a good partner, even in divorce Δ When you are "wrong", admit it … own it … accept it. Then move on Δ One of our common struggles is to learn to not do what comes "naturally" to us and to do what we have learned is healthy and correct Δ **Practice, practice, practice** Δ Do not commit to what you will resent doing Δ **All behavior has consequences** Δ Let go of outcomes (trying to control results). Δ Emotional pain is the barrier we must breech to have more choices in our lives and to grow toward our fullest potential Δ **The future does not exist**, so there is no way that you can actually know what will happen Δ **Decide what YOU want** Δ Stop asking your partner "Why" questions. These always start with an assumption which keeps us from really hearing! Δ **If you come ready for a fight, you will, most likely' get one** Δ Our pain gives us the ability to empathize Δ AFGO: another fucking growth opportunity Δ **Cry when you feel like it** Δ Accepting a gift is giving a gift Δ Things that our partners say that evoke strong reactions in us are keys to our issues and growth areas **△** Avoid **ACIDS**: **A**dvise, **C**riticize, **I**nstruct, **D**irect or be **S**arcastic **△** Honor your core commitments and choices **△** Any basic assumption that you have that seems to have a lot of emotion and defensive energy around it needs to be looked at and questioned **△** You can feel and keep your mouth shut – Bob **△** When training animals, desired behavior is rewarded, undesirable behavior is ignored. This works with humans, too **△** People tend to "go bad" when they feel criticized, powerless and unimportant. **△ It is always a good time to stop fighting... △** When we change ourselves, our environment changes **△** Respect yourself **△ Fear** – the common root of most of our undesirable behaviors **△** We will always be tested and sometimes we will fail. **△ If you don't ask, you will never get! △** There is no shame in having weaknesses **△ Being happy is important! △** Spouses want to respect their partners: be honest thus be forthright; have good, healthy boundaries **△** Use your past to learn. Change the behaviors and beliefs that don't serve you **△ Your perspective is *your* perspective. It is not objective reality △** Allowing another person to abuse you by accepting, condoning, inspiring or accepting their behavior is self – abuse **△** Dis-allow abusive behavior(s) in your relationship(s) **△ Agreements must be kept ... or mutually renegotiated △** Fixing the other person never works **△** When your partner doesn't hear you, perhaps you are answering the wrong question **△** The voice in your head that tells you that "you don't have to take this shit" is a sign that you need to listen very carefully to the other person, acknowledge your own fear and, perhaps, mirror and dialogue **△** Intent and impact are often polar opposites, when it happens acknowledge the impact that your words and deeds have on others. Don't retreat to the defense of what you "meant". Take responsibility for the impact of your words and create safety for the other person **△ Try evolving... △** Don't work out your "stuff" on or with your kids **△** It feels good to be in the presence of someone who is honest about themselves without trying to justify their behavior Δ "I love you" can be a lot of things including a question, a bludgeon and a sincere expression of affection. Δ Self-knowledge is power Δ Never underestimate the need for and the impact of a father in child's life Δ **Be the parent with your kid**(s) Δ Notice what pushes your buttons and refrain Δ As relationships deepen, the 'de facto' fears and insecurities will surface and need to be addressed Δ It is okay to admit to being overwhelmed and to ask for a little time to process Δ If the problems from one relationship crop up in another you missed an opportunity to grow Δ The stories we tell ourselves about others block communication, hearing and understanding. They leave no room for other people's realities Δ **Give up judgment and the need to be right** Δ Authenticity begins with self-honesty Δ Growth happens in "spurts". Stay with it and the spurts will happen. Δ Do not use the children to communicate with other adults Δ When a woman displays *rage* and *anger* it is because she feels safe enough to do so. Give her the opportunity to let her go through her anger to healing Δ Change is fear's greatest fear! Δ Love can be given endlessly without depletion Δ **Anger is an invitation to dialogue** – Sulaiman Δ Life is a "Lab" – you must experiment and take the information you gather from the reactions of others and use it to grow Δ Your anger is a "stressor" Let go of anger and you relieve some of your stress! Δ **Question your most deeply held beliefs!** Δ As men, it is up to us to seize the opportunities to make the first move in communication and dialogue Δ **Fixing other peoples stuff actually breaks it further** Δ If you feel anger or irritability, look for what it is you 'fear' underneath the feeling Δ We judge others by our own motivations: the assumptions you make about others often say more about you Δ **It doesn't matter what you're called, but rather what you respond to** – Sulaiman Δ All relationships that help us grow are successful Δ **Relationship Management Is Not Easy** – Hunt Δ It is okay to want something. It is not okay to insist that another person

184

provide that thing **Δ** **If you want to know what someone wants or what they think...ask them!** **Δ** What someone else thinks about you is none of your business. **Δ** **All endings are also beginnings** **Δ** It is all about you. You are the problem, you are the solution, you are the reason! **Δ** **Children learn from the behaviors of their parents** **Δ** That to which we react with anger and/or fear are the issues with which we truly need to deal **Δ** It is brave to take responsibility **Δ** Man, husband and father first. Business and other stuff after that

APPENDIX C

Angelique and Throg

This is a parable because it popped straight out of my head so consider my absolute lack of advanced degrees in biology and anthropology and take it with a healthy dose of salt. Still and all, however, it's a pretty good theory and it seems to explain a lot[72].

Some say that when a woman loses sexual interest in her spouse she will never regain it. I don't know if that's true, but I've seen plenty of anecdotal evidence to support it. Since the women involved are not crazy, and assuming there is no medical cause, there has to be has to be a rational explanation for what's going on

Back in the day, when we were just forming social clans of hunter gatherers there wasn't a lot of deep thought going on and it would be fair to say that almost all social interaction between the sexes found its origins in the mammalian brain and the

---

[72] Keep in mind I also have a theory that explains all the apparent inconsistencies of Gilligan's Island.

reptilian stem. Guys and dolls of Pliocene epoch, like the guys and dolls of today, relied upon unconscious stimuli and a million years of evolutionary conditioning when selecting and wooing their mates.

For the sake of argument, we are going to limit these fundamental attractions as follows:

Men are fundamentally attracted to fertility (youth) and health. Physical attractiveness is a factor as well, because it suggests genetic stability: from a preservation of the species point of view, congenital deformities are a sexual turn off.

Women are attracted to strength, social standing, and the ability to provide, and ditto on the attractiveness. It makes sense, because one, food was always an issue, and two, it doesn't do any good to select a mate based on his good looks if he isn't strong enough, or violent enough, to stop the rest of the gene pool from having at you.

Social standing equates into first, the ability to do what the guys do well, which was smashing in the heads of antelopes, and second, generating respect among the peer group, which was effected by smashing in the heads of the peer group.

Thus, cavemen self-selected by the ability to be violent. The violent aggressive guys not only brought home the antelope, but they killed off the weakling caveboy competition and got the hot babes. In all fairness, being violent was an essential survival skill for your basic male Homo Erectus.

Some time after Grog brought an antelope carcass back to the dwelling-site he caught an eyeful of Angelique, and she was, by Pliocene standards, hot. She probably had the majority of her teeth, she was disease free, and there was something about her that got him popping, maybe it was the shape of her face, the slope of her forehead, maybe it was hormones and pheromones; Grog didn't put a lot of thought into it. He lived in the moment, and he wanted Angelique in the worst way.

Angelique got a charge out of Grog and the masterful way he handled a club, she was attracted to his power and liked the thought of sharing his antelope... so to speak. So they yielded to their desires, bonded, and mated. So far, so good. They are in romantic love, and inevitably Angelique will become pregnant.

But there is another aspect of the biological imperative, there is another key to the survival of the species, and that is known as an energetic and diverse gene pool. Homo Erectus is never going to get to become Homo Sapiens without a lot of evolution and that requires mixing up the DNA as much as possible and that's not going to happen if Angique and Grog mate for life. Nature has to have a way of getting Grog out of one cave and into another.

And violence/fear is the answer. When Angelique was first attracted to Grog, one of the things she liked was his ability to smash skulls. Heretofore that had been a reason to avoid Grog altogether: a young cavegirl didn't grow up to be a cavemom if she got her head bashed in. Yet under the stupefying intoxication of hormones and pheromones, she forgot her fear and he was actually tender, for a caveman, and gentling. As long as they are in romantic love, she's not afraid of Grog and he's not inclined to smash her head. This is a win/win for the biological imperative.

But just like you and me and the rest of humanity, come eighteen to twenty-four months the body stops producing the chemicals that cause the intoxication we call romantic love, and in the cave it looks like this for Angelique and Grog:

She has recovered from the rigors of pregnancy and her infant, which she is genetically pre-dispositioned to adore, has been weaned and is less of an encumbrance on her, and suddenly Grog's violent behavior is less and less attractive and more and more of a threat to her safety, and more importantly to her baby's safety. She's not stupid. Infanticide is common in the animal world and children can be good eating when the antelope aren't running. Grog may or not be thinking about baby satay or even changed his behavior, but Angelique begins to perceive him, based upon her past experience of him and other cavemen and their head bashing ways, as a threat.

Angelique starts to cool towards Grog, and Grog, who doesn't understand, turns to the one social skill he has, violence, to get the one thing he wants, sex, and that causes Angelique to shut down completely.

Finally, Grog figures if he's not getting it in his own cave he'll get it somewhere else, and one day he comes back from the hunt and throws the antelope at Charlene's feet, and that's just fine with Angelique, who in a year will be making eyes at some other fine prehistoric boytoy.

The end result of all this is that Grog fathers a lot of children by a lot of women, and Angilique bears a lot of children by a variety of men, and the gene pool gets as turbulent as the olympic pool at the country club during free swim.

Which is a good thing, else we wouldn't be here and doing this, but at some time we have to let go of the anger and the fear. We have to grow past our genetic programming. We have to evolve.

Now, before you get your panties in a wad I am not saying you are violent, nor am I saying your wife is a paranoid gold digger.

But I want you to remember that Angilique started backing off from Grog when she didn't feel safe. NB: when she didn't feel safe. I submit that just as cavemen self-selected for violence, cavewomen self-selected for an ability to disassociate themselves from any perceived threat, i.e. fear.

Angelique identified violence as head bashing and baby eating. She probably didn't think of a backhand by Grog as particularly violent, nor would she think of rape anything other than foreplay.

And by Grog's standards, you are probably not a violent man. You don't routinely pummel herbivores to death, bash in the head of a male rival, or eat children, but the fact that you are a nice guy doesn't mean that your wife feels safe around you.

And I suspect that if your wife doesn't feel safe, she doesn't want to make herself vulnerable, and none of us are more vulnerable than when we are naked and in the arms of another. So if she doesn't feel safe, you aren't having a good sex life.

So what makes her feel less safe: sarcasm; anger; moral or intellectual superiority, belittlement, emotional blackmail; passive aggressiveness; disdain; contempt.

And this isn't to say that you are being sarcastic, angry, disdainful etc… it's just to say she interprets your behavior that way and feels threatened. Perhaps you are that way, perhaps it's projection on her part, more than likely it's a little of each.

So if you want to get you sex life back on track the key is for her to feel safe… and that means you must avoid the behaviors that allow her to feel unsafe and to practice the behaviors that allow her to interpret your otherwise unobjectionable behavior as safe.

Now you say to yourself: *Why is this my job? She's the one projecting her irrational and unrealistic fears onto me. She's the one that's having the atavistic flashback, she's the one that's letting her reptilian stem destroy our perfectly fine cerebral cortex relationship.*

And the answer is: because you are here, because you are the one learning how to row the boat. You can't talk her out of an irrational fear any more than you can talk her out of a rational fear. Don't try. You have the tools to change this relationship and you either use them, or the relationship ends.

So what does that look like? Try this on for size: a lot of guys feel that they have a right to sex, and that if they are not getting sex in the marriage there is something fundamentally wrong in the universe. Most guys look down, see an erection and say "SEE? I'M DOING MY PART! WHY CAN'T SHE DO HER'S?" and that comes across in everyday life as blame. Follow the logic: 1) sex is a right. 2) we're not having sex. 3) I always want to have sex. 4) You never want to have sex, ergo it is your problem, your bad.

So, if you think about it, your seductive style has changed over the years from. "How you doin?[73]" to "It's your fault."…. and you wonder why you're not getting any.

Add to that, guess what? She doesn't know why the switch is flipped. She feels, at some level, as you do, that she should want to be having sex. She feels guilty as hell already, and you adding your blame on to it not only doesn't help, but probably kicks in all her defensive skills, which are presently limited to anger and retribution.

---

[73] Joey Tribbiani, Friends, Warner Bros. 1994-2004

Suddenly by her lights this is her experience: *all you want is sex; you can't just cuddle; everything has to end with you between my legs and can't you please give me a break?* And when you don't, her defensiveness kicks in and she has to find a reason to blame you for her unconscious behavior, ergo: *You disgust me...*

I don't know. Maybe this isn't your reality, but I'm betting it is.

So how do you get your sex life back on line?

Well, clearly everything you've been trying hasn't worked so give all that a rest. Stop begging, stop blaming, stop demanding, just stop everything and get back to basics.

Remember when you were first dating? The odds are you're first words were not "Was that good for you?" You built up to it, you gained her trust, you made yourself vulnerable to her. So try that. Try going to your wife and saying something like

YOU: **Mary, I've been struggling with our sex life and our lack of intimacy. I remember how wonderful it used to be for us and I want to get back to that, but I know that I've done a lot in the past that's been destructive to our relationship and our intimacy and I am truly regretful and sorry for that. I've resolved to change a lot of things about me, and this is one of them. So I want to tell you now first, I don't blame you for our sex life. We've clearly drifted apart and I own my part in that. Second, I want to tell you that I love you, I adore you and I want to be with you for the rest of my life. Third, I want sex to be part of our relationship again, but I also know it's going to take time for us to get there and that's good by me. It's worth waiting for.**

And then you do all the stuff in this book. Simple enough, huh?

But also you do this: you initiate simple affection.

> A hug every morning and every evening… and make it
> last ten or fifteen seconds.
> Hold hands when you walk… in public. At the mall, at
> the grocery store. At church.
> Get out of the lazy-boy and onto the sofa: sit beside her.
> Touch her on the shoulder or face before you go to
> sleep.
> Stroke her hair.

Do not grab a tit or run your hand up her leg or do anything to initiate sex. Just don't do it. 1) it won't work and 2) it will just bring back all the bad thoughts she has about you in her head. She's going to think: *HERE WE GO AGAIN*. And you are back to square one.

And it may be that initially she is going to refuse. This is a change and change is scary so she will be resistant. She's going to think you are insincere; she may say you are being silly: but don't worry, and keep on working the system.

Don't give her a foot rub, offer her a foot rub… "you look tense, could you use a shoulder rub…" Invite intimacy, don't demand it.

You know how to do this: it's how you used to get laid. But the truth of the matter is you are now dealing with someone who has bad experiences with you… what used to take three dates and a foot rub is going to take months. Before you just had to win her affection, now you have to ease her atavistic fears and then regain her trust. She's got a lot of bridges to rebuild. It's going to take her time to get her trust back, and when it happens, the sex will come naturally.

And when it does (write this down) you are probably going to do something really stupid immediately afterwards that will fuck it all up. Change is hard, and the two of you are where you are because you both are, in some degree, comfortable with the hell you have endured for the past few years. When you start seeing your sexual relationship improve somewhere deep in your reptilian stem an alarm is going to go off because change is dangerous and you will do something stupid to restore the status quo.

The good news is that you will have gone about forty steps forward and just a few back, and you will, with practice and commitment, restore your relationship. I shit you not.

About the Author

Hunt Brown lives in Atlanta where he resides in the Little 5 Points community. He is a graduate of Emory University School of Law and his practice focuses on divorce mediation. (Gooddivorces.com) He is currently training to be an Imago Certified Teacher.

He can be reached at Hunt@gooddivorces.com or chb3@charleshuntbrown.com